WONDERS OF CREATION

Editors
Robert Pearman
Meryl Fergus
Pat Alexander

Picture research
Richard Atwill

Graphics
Tony Cantale
Nicholas Rous

Published by
Lion Publishing
121 High St, Berkhamsted,
Herts, England

Copyright © 1975 Lion Publishing

First edition 1975
Reprinted 1976
ISBN 0 85648 037 1

Printed in Britain by
Purnell and Sons Ltd, Paulton

Contents

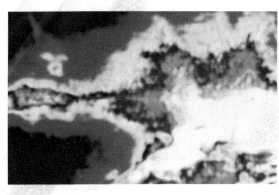

Contributors

Ernest C Lucas, MA, PHD
Research Fellow in Organic Chemistry at the University of Oxford, and Research Associate, Department of Biochemistry, University of North Carolina; then at Regents Park College, University of Oxford Department of Theology.

Hazel C Lucas, MA, PHD
Former Research Fellow, Department of Physics, at the University of Kent, and Research Associate, Department of Chemistry, University of North Carolina.

Colin A Russell, MSC, PHD, FRIC
Reader in the History of Science and Technology at the Open University, Milton Keynes.

George S Cansdale, BA, BSC, FLS
Formerly Superintendent of the London Zoo; has worked on numerous animal programmes on television for many years.

David A Hillson
Student of Biochemical Microbiology, University of Kent.

Barbara Drake
Teacher of Biology at Charterhouse Girls' School, Orpington, Avonbourne Girls' School, Bournemouth and Trinity School, Carlisle.

Malcolm B Waldron, PHD, FIM
Dean of the Faculty of Mathematical and Physical Sciences, University of Surrey. Former Senior Principal Scientist at the Atomic Energy Research Establishment, Harwell, responsible for research on nuclear materials.

F Nigel Hepper, BSC, MIBIOL, FLS
Principal Scientific Officer, The Herbarium, Royal Botanic Gardens, Kew.

Timothy J Stevenson, MA, DPHIL
Engineer working on computer memory devices, following research in Atmospheric Physics at the University of Oxford.

Morag L Ellison, BSC, PHD
Lecturer at the Institute of Cancer Research, London.

In the beginning

Ernest C. Lucas

This century has been a great age of discovery. Never has so much been found out about the world in which we live. Man has set foot on the moon, and is reaching out beyond.

But the more we know, the more we find there is to know. As scientists come to realize how complex the universe is, and yet how orderly it is, many have come to the conclusion that it cannot have come about by accident.

'In the beginning God created the heavens and the earth.' This is how the Bible opens its ancient account of the origin of all things. Do we know more than this? How did it happen?

The other chapters of this book describe many wonderful different aspects of the world – from the smallest living creatures to the huge planets that we have only just begun to explore.

But first we must set the scene. How, where and when did life begin? How did the world, the universe itself, begin?

An expanding universe?

Man's study of the universe has shown that it consists of a vast number of star systems, called galaxies, each of which contains many millions

Sunrise from space. An eclipse of the sun taken from Apollo 12. The earth has come between the spacecraft and the sun, blocking out its light except for a narrow rim.

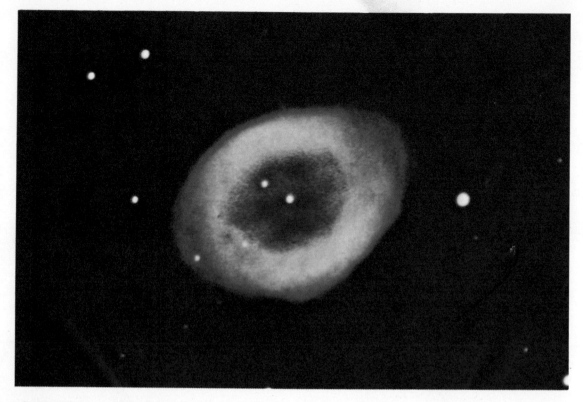

The Ring Nebula in Lyra Messier 57. The ring is formed by gases thrown off by the star in the centre.

of stars. The remarkable thing is that each galaxy is getting further and further away from all the others.

To put it another way, it seems as if we are living in an expanding universe.

One way of illustrating this is to paint a number of black dots on a balloon and then blow it up. As it expands each dot gets further and further away from its neighbours.

Two theories have been suggested to account for this expanding universe. According to one of them, as the universe expands more matter comes into being, so that the average amount of matter in any volume of space remains the same. This is called the 'steady-state' or 'continuous creation' theory. At first sight it might seem to suggest that the universe never had a beginning. It might always have been expanding, with new matter being created all the time. However, God could create a 'steady-state' universe, and then to anyone studying it after its creation it would appear not to have had a beginning.

A big bang?

Most astronomers today believe that the evidence favours a different theory. This is called the 'big bang' theory. According to this, there was once a time when all the matter in the universe was concentrated into a quite small, very hot, ball. This exploded and as the pieces flew apart they cooled down and first of all formed atoms, then clouds of gases, and then galaxies.

This theory says that the universe did have a beginning, but of course it says nothing about the origin of the matter out of which the universe is made. On the basis of what the Bible records, many believe that God created matter and formed the universe out of it, whatever kind of universe it might be.

If it is left to itself, will the universe continue expanding for ever? Scientists cannot yet answer that question. It depends on the amount of matter there might be in the universe. If it is less than a certain amount the answer would be 'Yes'. If there is more matter than this the attraction of gravity between the galaxies will be enough to cause the expansion to slow down and stop. The universe will then start to contract and end up as it began, as a fiery ball of matter.

The medieval view of heaven, from a woodcut.

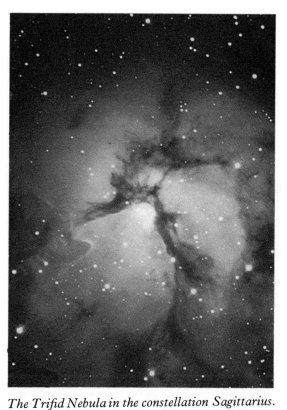

How did our planet earth begin?

We have seen how the universe might have come
to be like it is now. What about the origin of our
own planet earth? Several theories have been
suggested to explain this.

It seems very likely that the origin of the earth
is linked with the origin of our local star, the sun.
There is evidence that stars are born in the great
clouds of dust and gas which exist in our galaxy.
One such cloud, the Orion Nebula, can be seen
with the aid of a good pair of binoculars or a
small telescope.

It is possible that our solar system, the sun
and its nine planets, began as a cloud of gas and

*The Trifid Nebula in the constellation Sagittarius.
A shimmering cloud of gas and dust 12,500
million million miles away within the Milky Way.*

dust. Gravitational attraction caused it to contract, and as it did so it also began to rotate
faster and faster. The combination of contraction
and rotation would result in a dense ball of gas,

How a star is formed

*An eddy current (like a
whirlpool) is set up within
a nebula, leading to the
formation of a small
independent cloud of
gas called a protostar.*

*As matter at the centre
condenses due to
gravitational attraction it
spins faster to form a
star with a flat disc of
rotating matter around it.*

*Due to its contraction under
gravity, high temperatures
are created and eventually
nuclear reactions begin.
The star glows and then
shines brightly as the
temperature rises.*

*At the incredible
temperature of
14 million° C the
star is ablaze
and mature.*

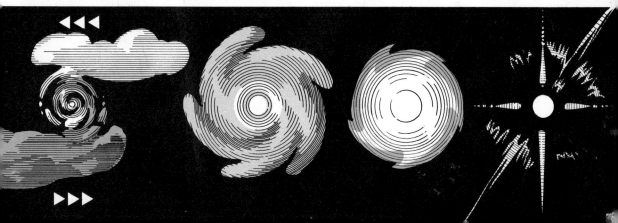

the sun, surrounded by a flat ring of gas and dust around its equator. The planets would be born out of this ring, by a process similar to that which produced the sun.

If it was formed in this way, the earth would have begun as a cold mass of dust, ice and gas. However, as it contracted under the influence of gravity, and as energy was released by radioactive elements, it would warm up. There is evidence that the earth passed through a molten stage and then cooled down again. As it began to cool it probably had a very foggy atmosphere of dust, water-vapour and other gases. On cooling, the water-vapour condensed and eventually the water fell as rain to produce rivers and oceans. In time the atmosphere would clear and become like it is today.

Genesis and science

How are we to relate the creation story of the first chapter of Genesis to the theories of the scientists? To begin with, it is very important to realize that the Bible's account was never intended to be a scientific description of how things began. It was written to teach certain very important truths to its first readers, centuries before Christ, and to those who would read it after them. If it had been written in modern scientific terms it would have been quite meaningless to the ancient Hebrews, and the language might have been out of date by the year AD 2,000.

Genesis teaches that God created the universe. It did not happen by chance. God created a universe that was beautiful and attractive. When he looked at it he could say that it was good. Man was patterned on the likeness of God himself – with the ability to reason and choose and be creative. This makes him different from all other living creatures. He has been given the job of looking after the planet earth and all the life on it.

Compared with other ancient creation stories the Genesis account is very remarkable. These others are obviously imaginative inventions, and no-one would think of trying to compare them with a scientific description. But the Genesis story is so matter-of-fact and so close to modern

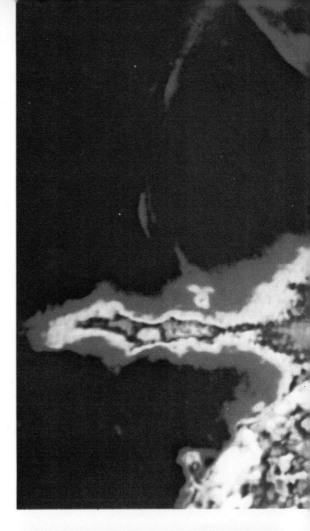

The spiral galaxy in the constellation Canes Vaenatici has about 100 million suns in its nucleus. This is how our own galaxy, the Milky Way, looks from space.

Hot rarified gases erupt to a height of 500,000 miles from the surface of the sun. Pictures from the orbiting skylab mission are colour-coded so that the composition of the sun can be studied in detail.

scientific accounts that it is tempting to try to relate the two.

For example, some people see in the first four days of creation a description of the earth as it cooled. At first it is a featureless planet with a thick covering of cloud through which sunlight cannot penetrate. Then (first day), the atmosphere clears enough for the difference between day and night to be noticed. Next (second day), the water vapour condenses to form clouds overhead and the oceans beneath. Finally (fourth day), the atmosphere clears enough for the sun, moon and stars to be visible.

It has also been pointed out that the order in which life is created in Genesis is the same as that suggested by scientists. Plant life is created first, next sea animals, then land animals, and finally man. These suggestions are interesting, but we must remember that scientific theories change, and so any attempt to relate the Genesis story to a particular theory will have its problems and will be incomplete.

When did life begin?

What about the origin of life itself? Most scientists believe in some form of evolutionary theory as the best explanation. They believe that the molecules that are important for life could have been produced from small molecules (such as water, carbon dioxide, ammonia, and methane) under the influence of sunlight, volcanic heat, lightning flashes, and cosmic rays. They then suppose that a series of lucky accidents led to the formation of a 'self-replicating' system, that is a collection of molecules that could produce a copy of itself. This was the first living cell. All creatures alive today are supposed to have descended from this first cell.

The characteristics of a living cell are

Galaxy NGC 4565 in the constellation Coma Bernca. From this side the Milky Way looks like this. Our sun is situated about 170,000 million, million miles from the centre of our galaxy, and near the central plane.

controlled by a large molecule which scientists call deoxyribonucleic acid (DNA for short). Each characteristic is produced by a small section of the DNA called a gene. When a living cell reproduces, it passes on a copy of its DNA to the new cell which it produces. Sometimes there is an error in the copying process and this results in a change in one of the genes. These errors (called mutations) can be caused by the presence of certain chemicals or by certain kinds of radiation.

If the change is a large one the new cell containing the mutated gene will not survive, because its whole life process will be thrown into confusion. But if the change is only a small one the cell will survive, though it will have some new characteristic not found in its parent cell. This new characteristic might be either an advantage or a disadvantage to the new cell.

Natural selection

What is true of single cells is, of course, true of those creatures made up of many, many cells. For example, suppose an animal which hunts at night has better night vision than usual, as the result of a mutation in the light-sensitive cells in the eye. That animal will be more successful in hunting. As a result it will be healthier and live longer than most of its kind. It will therefore produce more offspring than usual. Many of these will inherit its better night vision, and will pass it on. Consequently this new type of animal will gradually replace the older type whose night vision is not as good. If there is a period when food is particularly scarce, the

advantage will be especially valuable and the replacement process will be more rapid. This replacement process is known as 'natural selection'.

Many scientists believe that this combination of mutation and natural selection is what has produced all the present living creatures, in all their variety, from the original living cell. The principal piece of evidence they point to in support of this theory is the fossil record. Some rocks contain within them the fossilized remains of animals and plants which were alive at the time when the rocks began to form. In some cases it is possible to tell, by radioactive dating methods, how long ago the rocks were formed. When this is done it is found that, in general, the older the rock the simpler the forms of fossilized life it contains.

The oldest fossil-bearing rocks contain only single-cell creatures, such as bacteria. As the rocks get more recent they contain first many-celled sea creatures, then fishes, then amphibians (creatures that live both in water and on land), then reptiles (e.g. the dinosaurs), then mammals (warm-blooded animals) and finally man. It is argued that mutation and natural selection are responsible for the increasing complexity of living things as time went on.

Missing links

From a scientific point of view there are two main weaknesses in this evolutionary theory. First, there is no way of testing whether, over a very long period, mutation and natural selection could produce the very great changes needed – for example – to turn fishes into amphibians. Some scientists doubt this. They believe that only a number of relatively small variations, not new kinds of creatures, could be produced in this way.

Secondly, the fossil record does not prove that there has been a continuous process of development. It contains many gaps where the evolutionary theory would lead us to expect some intermediate type of creature, bridging the gap between two related types, one of which supposedly evolved from the other.

People who hold to the validity of the Bible are also divided in their attitude to evolution. Some believe that it is a plausible scientific theory and

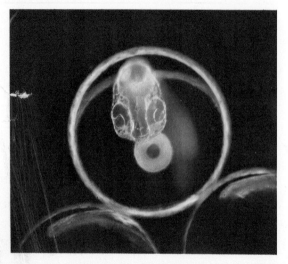

Life beginning in a single cell. An embryo develops within a fish's egg.

DNA – the blueprint for all living cells

A DNA molecule is composed of nucleotides. These are chemical combinations of sugar-phosphate and one of four bases, adenine, thymine, guanine or cytosine.

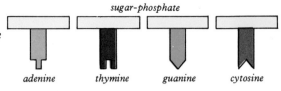

sugar-phosphate

adenine   thymine   guanine   cytosine

The bases in one strand of DNA can combine with those in another strand, forming what is called a double helix. Adenine can only combine with thymine and guanine only with cytosine. In this diagram they are shown as shapes that fit into each other. In fact they fit together by weak chemical bonds.

In a strand of DNA the nucleotides are arranged in a specific order. This order forms the blueprint that controls the production of all living things.

Each living cell contains chromosomes made up of the genes which dictate different physical characteristics. The 'blueprint' for making these characteristics is carried in the arrangement of the four nucleotides in the strips of DNA which form the genes.

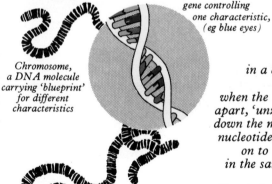

gene controlling one characteristic, (eg blue eyes)

Chromosome, a DNA molecule carrying 'blueprint' for different characteristics

DNA is reproduced in a cell as the cell divides. Reproduction begins when the two jointed bases pull apart, 'unzipping' the molecule down the middle. Free-floating nucleotides can then be joined on to the divided strands in the same order as before. The result is two identical molecules of DNA.

that it does not contradict the Genesis account. They point out that in Genesis it is said that the living creatures were produced out of the earth. This, they say, is also what the theory of evolution maintains.

All living creatures originate from the first living cell, which was formed out of chemicals produced on the surface of the earth in its earliest ages. They claim that mutation and natural selection has not been a chance process, but the means by which God brought into being things that he chose to make.

On the other hand, those who take the first chapter of Genesis as speaking of literal twenty-four hour days hold that God created all the different kinds of living creatures in the course of six days, a few thousand or tens of thousands of years ago. They believe that the fossil record was produced by Noah's flood.

Others hold a view that is mid-way between these two. They believe that the various different types of creatures have not all come from a single original cell, but that God created different types of living things at different times during the course of hundreds of millions of years. This, they claim, explains the two main characteristics of the fossil record – the apparent progression of increasingly complex forms of life and the missing links. Those who hold this view accept that some evolution has occurred, causing variations of the forms God created.

Man the manager

Although Christians hold different opinions over the method God used to bring life into existence, they all agree that the present forms of life are not here by pure chance. They are the result of God's activity. There is a meaning and purpose in their existence. God created man to reflect his own nature. This makes man different from all other living creatures. What is more, he has been given the job of looking after the planet earth and all the life on it, as God's deputy manager.

This does not mean that man has a right to do whatever he likes. He is not to rule the earth like a selfish dictator. It means he must look after it in a wise and loving way, remembering that the planet and all the living creatures on it are the work of the same God who created man himself. Since man is God's deputy he ought to treat the earth in the way God wants him to – God who is wise, just, and loving.

One of the greatest of all the wonders of creation is the fact that God has entrusted so much to man. Compared with the beauty and vastness of the night sky – God's handiwork – man seems so very insignificant. Yet God has given him pride of place in the universe, with authority over every living thing and a commission to put the world's resources to good use. Why should a great God like this bother with puny little man? Because of the greatest wonder of all: that God loves each one of us.

Evil in a good world?

But to stop there is to ignore the questions that still remain. If God loves his creation, including

A lion eating his prey. Not all nature is beautiful. In order to survive animals prey on each other.

An ant is caught in the sticky globules of a Sundew plant.

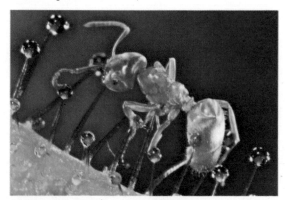

Typhoid bacillus seen under the electron microscope. These tiny living organisms carry a disease that can kill hundreds of people in an epidemic.

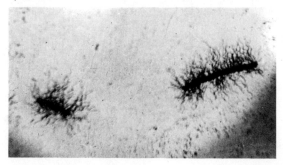

man, why is there so much in the world today that is not good? Why is there disease and suffering, hatred and war?

The chapters that follow the account of creation in Genesis have some vital things to say about the problem of evil.

Some see these chapters as a presentation of basic truths in a story form. 'Adam' is Hebrew for 'man' and 'Eve' Hebrew for 'woman'. So Adam and Eve represent the human race. Others take it more literally as the story of how the first ancestors of modern man disobeyed God and brought evil into the world.

The story of the Garden of Eden certainly has its roots in history. It is not just an imaginative fairy tale. Genesis 4 tells of a descendant of Adam called Tubal-Cain, who was the first person to use metal to make things. This means that Adam must have used only stone implements. Genesis 2 tells us that Adam was a gardener and that he tamed animals. All this adds up to a picture of Adam as what we would call a 'New Stone Age man'.

Now, as far as Europe and the Near East is concerned, the New Stone Age began around 8,000 BC in the upland plateaux of Turkey, and then spread into Mesopotamia, Palestine and Europe. What is interesting is that the Bible places the Garden of Eden in the area where the New Stone Age culture first arose. From the second chapter of Genesis it seems that Eden was at the place where the Tigris and Euphrates rise – which is in the upland plateaux of Turkey. In addition the word 'Eden' may come from a Babylonian word meaning 'plateaux'.

How the creation was spoilt

However we relate the second and third chapters of Genesis to the evidence and theories produced by the scientists, the important thing is to grasp what they say about the question of evil.

First, the world as God originally made it was good. The source of evil was outside this world and outside man. But it was man's rebellion against God which spoilt things. It brought an end to man's former free and happy relationship with God. It separated him from his Creator.

It also affected the whole created world. It caused disorder, disease, and pain. Every part of the world was infected by man's rebellion, from the tiniest cell to the largest plant. Men down the ages have continued to disobey and disregard God; and the natural world has taken its full

share of frustration, abuse and suffering in consequence.

However, since evil was not built into the world originally, we can be sure that it will be overcome and eventually removed. The central theme of the whole Bible is how God is going to bring this about by making it possible for rebellious man to return to a relationship of love, honour and obedience with his Creator.

New worlds for old

This book is about the wonders of the created world. But the chapters that follow will also highlight some of the frustration of a world that is not entirely in order or at peace with itself. We shall read about beauty and ingenuity but also about disease and destruction. This is where the rest of the Bible's message comes in, telling us about Jesus Christ.

God did not just write the world off when it went wrong. He did not destroy what he had made or leave it to work out its own salvation or destruction. Instead he made it possible for there to be a new start, and for the created world to be re-made and return to what he originally intended.

So God sent his Son, Jesus Christ, into the world. He became a man and lived a life of love and obedience towards God. At every point in his life he overcame evil. And when he was made to die on a cross as a criminal, he died the death due to all who had done wrong. He himself had never done anything wrong. He died to pay the penalty due to us, so what we do not have to suffer the final separation from God which we deserve.

What this means for the created world is that there will be a new heaven and a new earth. Paul described it in this way: 'In the end the whole of created life will be rescued from the tyranny of change and decay, and have its share in that magnificent liberty which can only belong to the children of God.' He said that Jesus came to bring a 'new creation'. For Jesus not only died, he rose again. The new creation he started then we can share already. But it will not be complete until the present 'old' creation is finally wound up, and all things are 'made new'.

We can be sure that the wonders of that new creation will be even greater than the wonders of the creation we see around us now, for that will be a world made new, free from all pain and evil, in which all creatures recognize and love God, their Creator.

Building-blocks of the universe

Hazel C Lucas

Suppose that a very brilliant scientist has invented a new machine and invited you to go with him on a new adventure – not a machine for travelling into outer space, but one that can make you smaller. Now you can explore the strange worlds which are all around us in the things we see every day.

If you are 4–5 feet tall and get into the machine and set the controls for one thousand times smaller, when the machine stopped you would be a millimetre or two high, about as big as an ant. You would be able to see how the spider spins his web, and how the mosquito's proboscis uncurls when he bites someone. You could visit a beehive, and see the workers arriving laden with pollen, the grubs being fed, and all the wonderful organization of a huge colony of insects working together.

If you visited a pond, you would be the same size as many strange little water-creatures bustling about their daily business of feeding, laying eggs, and escaping from their enemies. You would also be the same size as a lot of things that are not alive, grains of sand and tiny shells on the seashore, crystals of ice in a snowflake.

Where life begins

If you got into the machine again, and set the dial for another thousand times smaller, that is, a million times smaller than usual, you would find another world altogether, so different in fact that you probably would not recognize it. This is the world of cells and big molecules; tiny living things of great simplicity and big molecules of great complexity. It is the place where chemicals end and life begins.

You could travel in someone's bloodstream, and see the fight between the influenza virus and the antibodies that person's body makes to overcome the disease. You could watch the enzymes in his stomach digesting the food he was eating, systematically breaking down the big protein molecules. You could marvel at the intricate patterns of the long snake-like or twisted molecules that go to make up a plastic bag, a piece of expanded polystyrene, or one of the modern materials we use every day.

The world of the atom

If, after this, you took yet another trip in the machine, a thousand times smaller again, you would come to one of the strangest worlds of all, that of the atom. These are the building-blocks of which the whole universe is made.

You have probably seen pictures of what we think the atom looks like. It has a nucleus which is very dense, and so small that even though you were the same size as the atom, you could not see it. It is drawn larger in the diagram! Around the nucleus, like planets round the sun, fly the electrons in their orbits. They are a great deal smaller and lighter than the nucleus.

Really the whole atom, like the solar system, is mostly empty space. The number of electrons determines what sort of atom it is. For example, if there is one electron orbiting around a very small nucleus, the atom is hydrogen. Eight electrons around a slightly larger nucleus give oxygen. And a heavier nucleus, lead, is surrounded by a cloud of 82 electrons.

When you add electrons to atoms

Why do some atoms have more electrons than others? The answer to that lies in the nucleus. Each electron carries one unit of negative electricity. The nucleus contains some particles called protons, each of which carry one unit of positive electricity (it also contains some particles called neutrons with no electric charge).

If an atom is separated from all other atoms, there will be equal numbers of positive and negative particles, because they attract each other rather like the north and south poles of a magnet. The nucleus will attract just the right number of electrons so that the electric charges balance.

What would happen if you started adding

The composition of atoms

An atom of lithium. Three electrons move around the nucleus, which contains three protons and four neutrons.

○ neutron   ◐ proton   ● electron

Uranium is the most complex atomic structure with 92 electrons. The electrons travel around the nucleus in paths ('shells') that are confined to definite energy levels. These shells are given the letters K to Q as references and each shell can hold only a limited number of electrons.

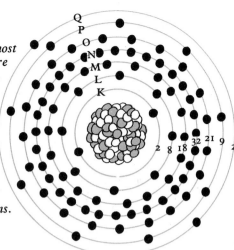

Q P O N M L K

2 8 18 32 21 9 2

hydrogen

nucleus +1 ○ positively charged

−1 ● electron negatively charged

helium

+2

−1
−1

neon

+10

−1 −1 −1 −1 −1 −1 −1 −1 −1 −1

A crystal of common salt

Common salt is a compound of sodium and chlorine, called sodium chloride. The electrically charged atoms, called ions, are arranged alternately in a cubic structure. This gives salt crystals their regular appearance.

These two diagrams are just different ways of visualizing the structure on paper. The lines in the second represent forces of attraction between the ions.

sodium

+11

chlorine

+17

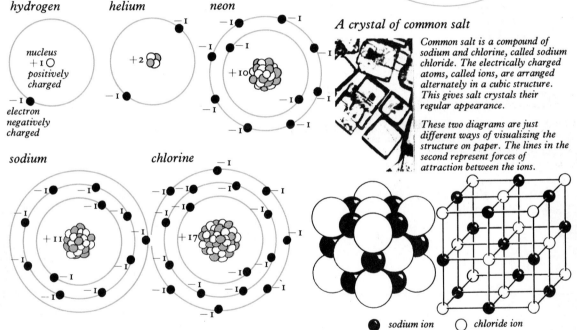

● sodium ion   ○ chloride ion

A synthetic detergent molecule

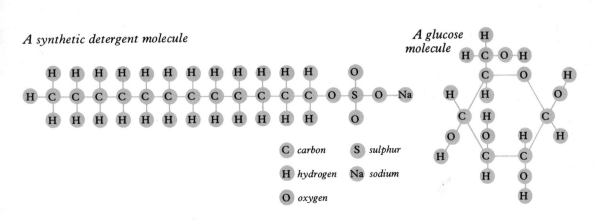

A glucose molecule

C carbon   S sulphur

H hydrogen Na sodium

O oxygen

more electrons to a hydrogen atom (and the same number of protons to the nucleus, of course)? What would the new atom look like? If you added one more electron (giving helium), you would find that the second electron went into an orbit very similar to that of the first electron. The two together make an electron 'shell' around the nucleus – no more electrons can get in.

The next electron would start a new shell, slightly farther away from the nucleus, and the second shell holds eight electrons. So you could build up more and more complicated atoms, filling up more and more shells, until you reached uranium, with 92 electrons. When the atom reaches about this size the nucleus is often

unstable and disintegrates on its own. This is what we call radioactivity.

Does it surprise you that by adding just one electron (and one proton) to an atom of neon (a light gas used in fluorescent lamps) we have an atom of sodium (a silvery metal)? How can one electron make so much difference? To answer this we must consider what happens when we bring two atoms close together.

Suppose we start with two neon atoms. Each has ten electrons orbiting around it, making two closed shells. A closed shell is very stable and so really nothing much happens when two neon atoms meet. The force of attraction between them is very small.

Now it is a universal rule that when particles get hotter, they move faster – vibrating, spinning round, or just rushing to and fro. The temperatures we live at are very hot from the atom's point of view. So the neon atoms are trying to move around, and there are only very small forces to hold them together. Nearly all substances are solids at very low temperatures, but at temperatures far below those we live at, the

If you were 1,000 times smaller, you might see a ladybird making a meal out of an aphid, or come face to face with a jumping spider with four eyes!

neon atoms break free from each other and wander round independently (which means they are a gas). All atoms with closed shells are like this. They are called inert gases because their atoms do not interact much with each other, or with anything else.

When atoms combine

At the opposite end of the scale, let's see what happens when a sodium atom (with two closed shells and one extra electron) meets a chlorine atom (with two closed shells and seven extra electrons, that is, the third shell is full but for one electron). If these two atoms combine, the sodium's extra electron can fill up the chlorine's third shell and both will be much more stable. This will mean that the sodium atom is left positively charged and the chlorine atom negatively charged. They will attract each other like the poles of a magnet. The forces between them are very strong, there is a chemical reaction, and they form common salt.

This is still a solid at the temperatures we live at. If you were to take a journey in the machine through a crystal of salt, you would find the sodium and chlorine atoms arranged alternately, as in the diagram, held very tightly together. Solids are nearly all more complicated versions of this diagram, with each atom staying in just about the same place in a regular pattern.

Other atoms can combine by sharing electrons. The electron orbits then go round two nuclei instead of one. The number of electrons each atom has and the shape of the orbits determine whether two atoms will combine to make a new substance; whether a substance is a solid, liquid, or gas; whether one thing dissolves in another, and a host of other questions!

Sometimes the spare electrons are so loosely bound to the atoms that when the nuclei form a solid, all the electrons are shared between all the nuclei. Such solids are called metals. The electrons each have a negative electric charge, and if we can make them move from one side of the metal to the other, we have created an electric current. Most of the electric gadgets we use every day work because electrons are flowing through a length of wire.

Holding things together

One of the most important atoms is carbon. It

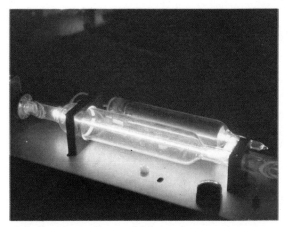

A helium-neon laser which produces an intense beam of red light by activating the electrons in the mixture of gases in the tube.

has six electrons – that is, one closed shell, and one half-full shell containing four electrons. The carbon atom can share its four spare electrons with four more carbon atoms arranged all round it, and each of these can share with the first atom and three others, and so on.

In this way whole chains of carbon atoms can be built up, with side chains and other atoms stuck on here and there. That is how the big molecules like proteins – the building-blocks of living things – are made. If it were not for the electrons holding the carbon atoms in our bodies together, we would disintegrate into millions of pieces!

Energy

Electrons have yet another property which is very important to us. Not only atoms, but electrons too, move faster when they get hotter. If they are heated, the outer electrons sometimes jump out of their orbits into more energetic orbits further away from the nucleus. Afterwards, when they jump back again, they give out light.

The sun has nuclear reactions going on inside it which give out energy. It is surrounded by clouds of gases which use the energy to send their electrons into higher orbits. When the electrons jump back again they give out that energy as light or heat – the forms in which it reaches the earth. So, if it were not for the electrons, life as we know it would be quite impossible.

How remarkable these little particles are. Their properties are such that they can build up the hundred or so completely different atoms which go to make up our universe.

Return journey

If the machine were to take you back again to the world of big molecules and cells, you would be amazed at the vast range of complexity that is possible when these atoms combine. Somewhere in the increasing complexity – though the dividing-line is hard to find – things stop being just substances and come to life.

Returning from the world of the cell to the world of insects, things are more complicated still. Here are communities of ants and bees, working away to lay their eggs, gather food and protect their young.

Set the dial again and you are back in the world of man. Now the complexity is so great that all kinds of wonderful things have happened.

Human beings do not just follow instincts like the ants. We can choose whether or not to co-operate. We can love, enjoy beauty, and know the difference between what is true and what is false. We can think about ourselves and the purpose of our lives. We can even share these things with one another. We are more than a collection of millions of atoms.

A helpful way to look at it is to think of a few letters. No matter how you arrange them they don't mean anything. If you have a few more, you can make some words. If you have more still, you can make sentences, and say something that means far more than just a few letters. It seems as if, as things get more complex, stages are reached when something new and more meaningful is created. So the Christian who is a scientist can say, 'We are made out of the dust of the earth.' Then he can also say in the next breath, 'We are made in the image of God.'

From simple to complex forms of life : a one-celled marine dinofugellate ; the beautiful pattern of an ephyra larva ; and a much more complex organism, Phyllosoma larva of squillid.

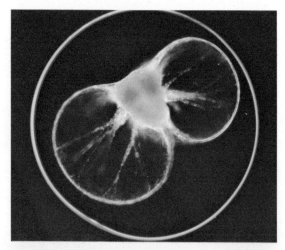

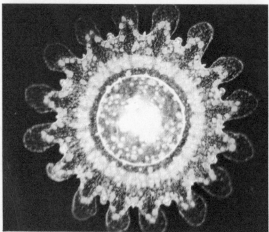

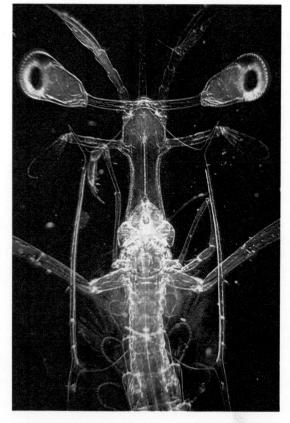

What is our universe made of?

Colin A. Russell

Could life exist in other parts of the universe than our earth? If we know what the rest of the universe is made of we can make better guesses about whether life like ours exists there.

We shall see in later chapters that air and water are essential for human life. While it would be quite wrong to suppose that God could only make life as we know it on earth, at least it would be good to know of any other places where our own conditions were repeated.

The sun

For many centuries people believed that the elements of which the planet earth was made were earth, water, air and fire, and that they were only to be found on the earth or very near it. From the moon outwards there was nothing but a fifth element called 'ether' (nothing to do with the modern anaesthetic of that name!).

The four terrestrial elements have not been taken very seriously for the last 400 or 500 years; and during that time the 'ether' has come under grave suspicion. But how could we prove anything about the composition of objects millions of miles away? About 100 years ago a new experimental method became available. The experiments were not of course done by ordinary laboratory examination of samples from outer space. Instead a new technique was used, known as spectroscopy. This makes use of the fact that light from many sources can be split up by special optical instruments into separate parts, just as white light is separated in the rainbow

Our blazing sun. The sun's energy is created in its core at a temperature of 16 million °C by a process which transforms hydrogen into helium. It continuously radiates into the atmosphere an astonishing $370,000 \times 10^{18}$ kilowatts of power.

This illustration from Dante's Divine Comedy *shows an early view of the nature of the universe. The earth is at the centre and the planets move on spheres around it.*

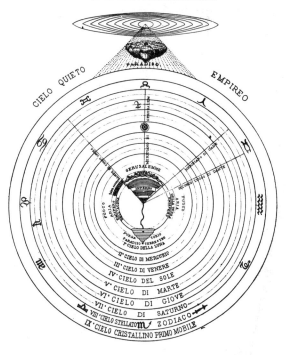

into seven or so colours. It is not hard to arrange a device in which the different wavelengths are recorded as lines in a *spectrum*. The nature of this spectrum depends on the wavelengths of the light, and these in turn depend on the chemical composition of the light source.

The different wave-lengths of the separated parts can then be measured. These will vary according to the chemical composition of the light sources. A spectroscopic examination of light from the sun or stars can therefore give us valuable clues about the chemicals present in them.

In the nineteenth century it became fashionable to examine with a spectroscope the light from the sun while most of it was covered during an eclipse. The evidence suggested that part of the sun's spectrum was due to hydrogen, well known as an element on earth. So much for the 'ether'!

Then, in the 1880s, the astronomer Norman Lockyer noted some features in the sun's spectrum which did not correspond to any known element on the earth. He called this 'helium', and for a while it looked as though the ancient philosophers might have been partly right in saying that the elements on the earth were quite different from those on the sun.

Some thirty years later, however, helium – despite its name, which comes from a Greek word meaning 'sun' – was located on the earth, and is now manufactured on a fairly large scale for filling balloons.

The stars

So it became clear that the earth and the sun, at least, are really made of the same kind of 'stuff',

or chemical elements. But what of those other luminous bodies, the stars?

Their light was examined in the same way and, although they are unimaginably great distances away from us, they were shown to be made of the same kind of chemical elements as those found in our own solar system. Examination of their light shows that they have well over 90 per cent of hydrogen, the lightest element known. It now seems fairly clear that hydrogen, and perhaps helium, are converted within the stars to other heavier elements. So far as our solar system is concerned, hydrogen and helium constitute about 98 per cent of all matter there.

If you ask why we do not have more of them on earth, the reply usually given is that the earth and some other planets were not big enough to retain them through gravitation and so, being very light elements, they escaped long before we came on the scene. Thus the earth is unusual in containing a high proportion of the other heavier elements – nitrogen, oxygen and many others, including the metals.

The planets

Our near neighbours in space include the planets, bodies which, like ourselves, encircle the sun. They do not shine by their own light, but merely reflect that of the sun. So we cannot use spectroscopy in the same way as we could for

The relative sizes of members of our solar system

There are several thousand minor planets between Mars and Jupiter, in what is known as the asteroid belt. Comets (the smaller fragments of which occasionally fall on earth as meteorites or burn up in the atmosphere as 'falling stars') and very small particles of dust which cause what is called the 'zodiacal light'.

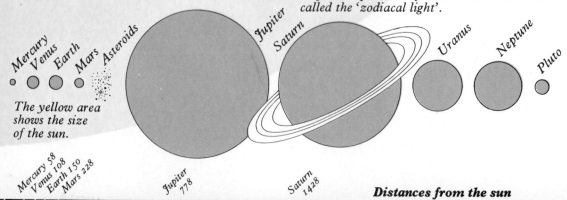

The yellow area shows the size of the sun.

Mercury 58
Venus 108
Earth 150
Mars 228

Jupiter 778

Saturn 1428

Distances from the sun

Uranus 287

the sun and the stars. But fortunately there are other techniques available.

One method of finding out what the planets are made of is to observe their orbits, or paths through space, very closely and to see how they vary with the approach of other bodies. This enables us to calculate the density of the planets and so to gain some notion of their composition. But what is really interesting about them is their atmospheres, and a great deal of evidence bears on this problem.

Of the five major planets known since ancient times (Mercury, Venus, Mars, Jupiter and Saturn), Jupiter and Saturn are the ones furthest out from the sun. They are incredibly cold and would seem to be totally inhospitable to any kind of life. Their atmospheres contain no oxygen but rather gases that act as its chemical opposites. We call them reducing gases (because they reduce, or take away, the oxygen from other substances) and they include hydrogen, ammonia and methane. The same observations have been made about the atmospheres of Neptune and Uranus.

The discs or rings around the planet Saturn are probably made up of millions of tiny particles. These are now thought to be solidified ammonia. This shows how cold it is, for ammonia does not solidify until very low temperatures are reached.

Coming nearer to the earth, we encounter the planet whose orbit is next to ours – Mars. This appears to have on its surface channels, which some have supposed to be artificial in origin. Other factors have also led many to speculate that there could be some form of life on Mars. For some time it has been known that, unlike the other planets, Mars has an atmosphere rich in carbon dioxide. Although it contains a lot of oxygen, that oxygen would not be available to life like ours. But it could conceivably nourish something like a plant. We are pretty sure that there is very little free oxygen on Mars, and there has been some doubt about whether there is much water.

In the early 1970s the spacecraft Mariners 6, 7 and 9 went near enough to the surface of Mars to obtain close-up photographs. Among many other interesting results emerging from these pictures is the nature of the 'snow' that covers the poles of the planet. It now appears that it is not ordinary snow (frozen water) but rather dry ice – solid carbon dioxide. This means not only that the polar regions must be much colder than our own, but that the atmosphere can contain very little water. This is worked out from rates of evaporation of the 'snow'.

This lack of water, more than the lack of oxygen, makes the possibility of life on Mars considerably more remote than was believed before these Mariner spacecraft set out. Of course the Mariner photographs brought no direct evidence of life; this would hardly be expected, as any living things on Mars must be extremely simple and small.

Now we come to our other neighbouring planet, the one next to us working inwards – Venus. It has been said that this is the nearest thing we have to a twin in space.

It is only slightly smaller than our own planet. Unlike the earth, Venus gives no evidence of oxygen or water vapour in its atmosphere, although carbon dioxide is certainly present. It looks to us like another 'burnt-out' world. And this is even more true of the planet nearest the sun, Mercury. One side of this is always facing the sun and is so hot that lead would melt and run like water; on the other side there is eternal winter and the sun never rises. It is unthinkably cold. The planet has very little atmosphere, so we would hardly expect life on Mercury.

The moon

Finally we must not forget our nearest companion in space, the moon. Needless to say, we no longer believe that it is made of green cheese! For quite a long time we have been sure that it has virtually no atmosphere. During an eclipse of the sun, when the moon comes between the sun and ourselves, its disc shows clearly against the bright background with no haziness at the edge, such as we would find if there was an atmosphere to blur the effect. Again, when the moon passes in front of a star, the star disappears instantly and sharply, without the blurring that would be caused if the moon had an atmosphere.

These and other facts have long convinced us on that point, and have ruled out almost all chance of there being life on the moon. But of

in millions of kilometres

Neptune 4498

Pluto 5898

Earthrise seen from Apollo 8 in orbit round the moon. The white swirls on the surface are cloud formations and the blue oceans can be seen between.

At last man actually walks on the moon. This spaceman is collecting specimens of lunar rock to bring back to earth for analysis.

course the Apollo missions to the moon have brought back many samples of lunar dust and rock. Now being examined in laboratories all over the world, these samples have given us a whole new range of insights into the moon's composition and possible origin. Indeed, even before the moon landings, unmanned spacecraft were able to send back information to earth concerning the moon's chemistry. Some of these early results are surprising, but it is too early to assert that many of the problems are solved.

Inter-stellar space

Now we go out into deep space again – not to any of the stars but to some of the unimaginably vast regions between them. We call these 'inter-stellar space'. For some time astronomers have known of the existence of clouds of gas and dust around the centre of our galaxy. They were supposed to consist of free atoms and sub-atomic particles. Thus, in 1968, came the dramatic discovery of the presence of that familiar molecule ammonia (NH_3), and in 1969 water was recognized in those remote depths of space. By now over a dozen substances common to any

A piece of lunar rock brought back by Apollo 12. Scientists all over the world have been working on the thousands of pounds brought back by the Apollo astronauts.

earthly chemistry laboratory had been identified in inter-stellar space, mostly by the new techniques of radio-astronomy. Some of these are simply organic substances like formaldehyde (CH_2O), and this has led some to suppose that life may have evolved from such humble beginnings in many other parts of the universe than here on earth. Other experts, however, are unconvinced, and the only honest attitude must surely be to 'wait and see'. The next few years should witness some exciting developments in this area.

The point of it all

During the last few years we have begun to take quite big strides forward in our understanding of the nature of matter beyond our earth. But what is the point of it all? Well, one reason is to enquire whether 'out there' are any conditions in which we might expect to find other living beings. Man has been puzzling over that one for

The planet Saturn. The unique rings of tiny particles are clearly visible and give Saturn its distinctive appearance.

hundreds of years. So far it looks as though we are uniquely situated on our earth, and there is not much chance of anything like animal life in our solar system. If we are wrong, and such life does turn up, it will be a fascinating discovery.

Fascinating, but not disastrous. Some Christians have often wondered if their faith would be in some way disproved by a discovery like that, and are glad when all the evidence seems negative. But their worries are needless. God has told us that he loved our human, earthbound race enough to send his Son to die for it – and that includes you, me and all other human beings. But he never told us that we were his only creation. Perhaps we were, in some sense. But God only tells us as much as we *need* to know – not to satisfy our curiosity. That is one of the jobs he has given to science.

So whether in the vast depths of space there are other creatures something like ourselves does not matter all that much. What does matter, as we lift up our eyes to the glorious night sky, is that we should be able to recognize that here is the handiwork of One who, though vast in power and knowledge, nevertheless loves and cares for every one of the wandering race of men.

Can these animals survive?

George S. Cansdale

Nowadays more and more wild animals are concentrated in the great National Parks, and in an increasing number of safari and wildlife parks.

This often means removing the animals from their natural environment and restricting their freedom to roam where they please. It may seem cruel. Yet, if conditions are good, these are the lucky ones. For they are safe from the worst of all their enemies – man himself.

Take the lion, for example. In the safari park he can live in safety. There are no big-game hunters, no guns, snares and traps. There are no food shortages, either. Yet on the plains of West Africa, where lions were common once, they are now seldom seen.

The disappearing lion

Centuries ago there were wild lions in every country from India right through to the southern tip of Africa. They were well known in Greece at the time of Alexander the Great and when all the stories about Ulysses and other ancient heroes were being written.

They were just as common in Palestine. David – who later became king of Israel – keeping watch over his father's sheep, had to protect them from hungry lions as well as bears.

Lion-hunting was a favourite pastime of the kings and nobles of ancient Babylon. They used special breeds of large dog to hunt wild lions. Some kept lions as pets in what was rather like a zoo. They even trained some lions to help hunt deer and antelope. You may remember how King Darius had the prophet Daniel thrown into his 'lions' den'.

Animals at risk

Today the situation is very different. The wild lions disappeared from most of these lands long ago, and now they can only be found in parts of Africa and in one tiny corner of India. Even there they are mostly in the safety of National Parks and Nature Reserves.

Although lions are much rarer than they once were, there is probably little risk of them becoming extinct. But other members of the big cat family (the leopard, for instance, and especially the tiger) are now on the danger list – something that would have seemed quite unthinkable twenty or thirty years ago.

Whose fault is it?

How has it happened? Who is to blame? The real answer is that we all are! The human race

has become a real threat to the survival of these animals. It all began long ago. As populations have increased, more and more land has been occupied, leaving less and less for the wild animals.

Animals that seemed dangerous and a threat to cattle, sheep and even to people, were treated as enemies and simply killed. Take Britain for example. Until about a thousand years ago, not long before William the Conqueror reached the English coast, there were brown bears living in the forests and mountains – not many, it is true, but they were firmly established. Wolves, however, were very common. Being much smaller and able to move around and hide more easily they survived much longer than the bears. There were still a few existing in the wilder parts of Scotland until about 200 years ago.

Today wolves are becoming rarer and rarer – even in countries like Russia and parts of North America, which have always had great packs of wolves roving around, and which did not seem to be much affected by man's attacks.

This may seem to be a good thing, because we think of wolves as cruel destroyers of other animals. But in fact these wild animals are not as cruel as man, for they kill their prey quickly. Indeed animals such as wolves are very useful. It would be a bad thing for many other species – deer and antelope, for example – if they became extinct.

Are animals cruel?

Nature is very complicated, yet each animal fits into its place and has a particular purpose. What we wrongly describe as the 'cruelty' of a wild animal may in fact save many other animals from suffering.

When wolves need food, they will attack the slowest animal in a herd, perhaps one that has injured itself and is already suffering, or one that has some disease. Without the marauding wolves, the injured animal would linger on, getting weaker and weaker until it died. Similarly a sick animal, if there were no wolves around, could infect and cause the death of others in the herd.

Although this may sound rather strange, it is better and healthier for these herds to be moved around and mixed up by the wolves from time to time. Otherwise they might just stay in one area, spoiling the ground.

It is a mistake to try to put ourselves in the animal's place and imagine how we would feel. In the National Parks of Africa, for instance, you can see lions and cheetahs wandering around, or just sitting, quite close to impalas, gazelles and other antelope. Far from being worried by the presence of these big cats, the other animals will just enjoy the grass. Of course they will keep an eye on the lions – sometimes posting a sentry for the purpose – and at the first alarm they will run, though not very far, before starting to feed once again.

They seem to live for the moment, with little thought of what has just happened or what might soon happen. They do not imagine things. The power of imagination and the ability to plan is one of the major ways in which we humans differ from the rest of the animal world. But we do not always use these gifts as we should, to exercise responsible care for the creatures God has given us charge over.

Animals in danger of extinction

These beautiful and powerful animals are now in danger of extinction.

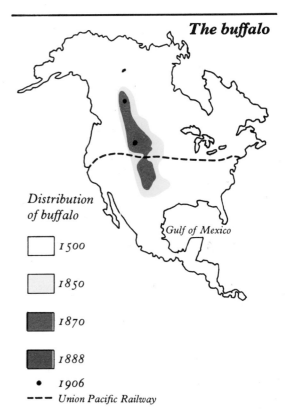

The buffalo

Distribution
of buffalo

☐ *1500*

☐ *1850*

■ *1870*

■ *1888*

● *1906*

- - - Union Pacific Railway

Gulf of Mexico

The effect of the railway line shows clearly that it is man who is endangering the life of the buffalo.

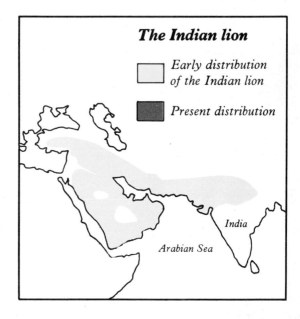

The Indian lion

☐ Early distribution
of the Indian lion

■ Present distribution

India

Arabian Sea

Why should we care?

Until relatively recent times human beings – generally speaking – have behaved as unthinkingly towards the created world as any animal. Man's greed, carelessness or vanity has led to the extinction of many animal species – the most famous being the dodo, long since 'dead'. Our greed continues to lead us into wholesale slaughter of animals for food. We drive them out of places that we want, with no thought of the consequences. And in our vanity we encourage hunters to shoot beautiful animals such as the leopard so that we can make their skins into coats – although there are other attractive and far less destructive ways of keeping warm.

We have been born into a world of variety and beauty. We enjoy watching the animal life against a colourful background of plants, landscape and sky. We still use the old-fashioned word 'creatures', which should remind us of the Creator who made all that is.

The law God gave to his people the Israelites through Moses over 2,500 years ago contains clear instructions about two problems we think of as modern – conservation and animal welfare. Although the people under Moses' command were travelling back from Egypt through desert country, where food was scarce, they were told – for example – that if they found a bird's nest they could take the eggs or babies for food but were to let the parent birds go free, so that they could nest again.

The law also taught the proper treatment of animals. For instance, if a man found a cow stuck in a pit he was to bring it to safety, no matter

The Dodo (Didus ineptus) once lived in Mauritius. It had a large body and small wings that were useless for flight. As a result man hunted it to death and it is now extinct.

whether it belonged to a friend or to an enemy. He must also ensure that the cattle and sheep had their food and water, even if it had to be done at times when work was normally forbidden.

The farmer was told he must never harness a donkey and bullock together to draw his plough, because these animals walk quite differently. However carefully the carpenter might shape the wooden yoke that went over their shoulders, it was bound to rub sore places, hurting and harming one or other of the animals.

These instructions may sound primitive in our mechanized age, yet the principles behind them are as important now as they ever were. The increase in concern for conservation and the welfare of animals today has come too late for some species, and perhaps too late even for that great creature of the sea, the whale. Yet it is not too late for many other groups of animals that now stand on the brink of extinction. We need to rediscover the principles expressed in God's law in order to apply them to the present-day situation, for the proper care and protection of all God's creatures.

A relief from Nineveh, dated about 650 BC. Lion-hunts have been recorded from earliest times.

The smallest living creatures

David A. Hillson

We know that the world God has created is full of animals and plants of many different sizes, shapes and colours. But what do we mean when we talk of 'living creatures'? What characteristics must something have before we can say: 'This is a creature; it is living'?

Until the invention of the microscope, man knew of the existence only of creatures he could see with his own eyes: elephants and tadpoles, trees and weeds. But when he first looked down a microscope, he found a whole new world in miniature.

Living?

Those of us reading this book will claim (quite rightly!) that we are living creatures. Yet we do not make the same claim for the chair or floor beneath us. What then do we mean by 'living'? How can we say, for instance, that a tree is living, but that a wooden chair is not?

All living creatures have certain basic essential characteristics:

    they grow;
    they multiply and reproduce;
    they eat and get rid of waste materials;
    they breathe in some way or other (though not necessarily air);
    and they react to their surroundings.

Inevitably some of these characteristics are more obvious in one creature than in another. We cannot, for example, see a tree breathing or eating, yet we know that it does. We do not actually see the weeds reproduce, yet they soon manage to grow all over our lawns and flower beds!

Small?

The earliest microscopes were optical ones, using a system of lenses to form a magnified image of the object being studied. At first such an instrument was rightly considered a great step forward in science. It enabled men to see details

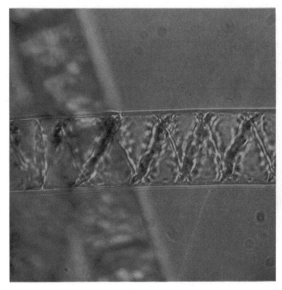

The simplest forms of life. Radiolaria are independent one-celled animals. They can move about by using their hair-like arms. Spirogyra is a simple plant commonly found on the surface of ponds. It can synthesize its own carbohydrates using its green chloroplasts.

How the electron microscope works

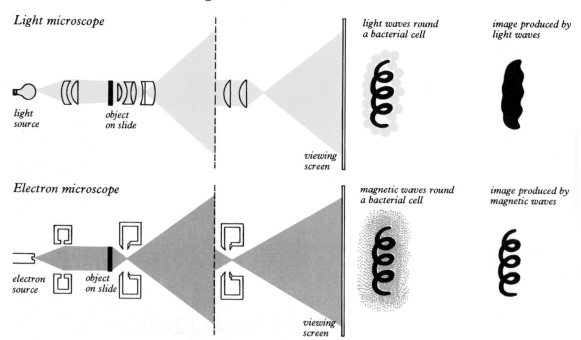

Light microscope

light source

object on slide

viewing screen

light waves round a bacterial cell

image produced by light waves

Electron microscope

electron source

object on slide

viewing screen

magnetic waves round a bacterial cell

image produced by magnetic waves

Both microscopes work on the same principle. In the light microscope, lenses focus rays of light to form the image.of the object. In the electron microscope, powerful magnets focus beams of electrons on to a photographic plate or special viewing screen. The smaller size of the magnetic waves gives a much clearer picture of the smallest objects.

so small that they had to invent a new unit of measurement (the micron – equivalent to one millionth of a metre).

But even more recent inventions have made the optical microscope seem no more than a relatively minor advance, as it can show nothing smaller than about a quarter of a micron. The electron microscope – in which a beam of electrons focused by means of an electronic lens, is made to form an enlarged image of an object on a fluorescent screen or photographic plate – can achieve a resolution one hundred thousand times as great as that of the optical microscope. This required the creation of a further unit of measurement (the Ångstrom – equal to one ten-thousandth of a micron). Using these instruments, scientists have been able to discover and examine a fascinating world of miniature creatures, so small that we can neither see nor feel them.

What are these creatures?

Some of the organisms discovered in this way

Preparing a glass slide for a microscope.

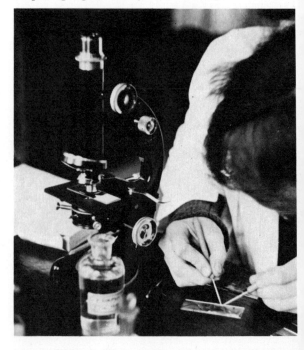

were given the names 'bacteria' and 'viruses'. These tiny creatures are popularly thought of as the agents of disease and illness, and bacteria and viruses are in fact often responsible. They cause colds and flu, for example. But before we condemn them all as harmful enemies, we should note that some are so important that without them human life could not continue.

Some bacteria are the principal causes of the decay of dead organic matter in the soil, helping to convert it into mineral substances from which plants manufacture their food. Others have an essential role to play inside the human stomach, where they ensure the successful digestion of the food we eat.

Whatever their function, these creatures are certainly very tiny. Bacteria have been found to measure from 0·01 to 5,000 microns in length, while viruses are from 200 to 3,000 Angstroms long. This means that it would take 20 million average-sized viruses put end to end to equal the height of a man 6 feet tall!

Bacteria at work

There are many different kinds of bacteria, but all of them consist of a single cell. They are divided into different groups or families mainly by their shapes.

Unlike plants and animals, bacteria do not have organs and tissues such as heart, eyes or legs. However, their internal structure is quite complicated, and can usefully be compared to the basic structure of a factory.

Inside every type of cell there is a control centre, known as the nucleus. (Some cells have more than one nucleus.) It contains information about how the cell is to be run, what it needs to produce, and other instructions – all written in code on long molecules called chromosomes, which are rather like the tapes for a tape recorder or computer. Bacteria have a single circular chromosome.

The factory workers

It would be no good, of course, if a factory had only a control room, with all the managers and foremen locked up inside! They need to have machinery with workers to operate it, as well as messengers to tell the workers what to do. This is exactly what we find in every cell, including bacteria.

The information on the chromosome is decoded and the message is then taken by another

How a living cell divides

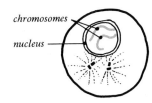

chromosomes
nucleus

1 Cell division begins in the nucleus of a cell when chromosomes, which are DNA, start to thicken.

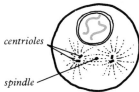

centrioles
spindle

2 As the chromosomes are thickening a spindle of fibres develops between two small 'asters' or centrioles.

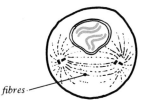

fibres

3 The fibres increase in number and each chromosome divides lengthways. The nuclear membrane begins to disintegrate.

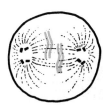

4 As the nuclear membrane disappears, the chromosomes attach themselves to the centre of the spindle. The chromosomes divide into pairs, followed by the division of the centrioles.

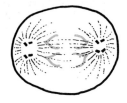

5 Half of each chromosome pair moves towards one of the pairs of centrioles pulled by the spindle fibres.

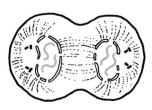

6 A nuclear membrane begins to surround the chromosomes of the new cells. The cell elongates and division of the cytoplasm begins.

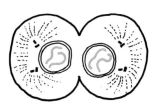

7 Cell division is almost complete. The fibres have disappeared and the two new cells are identical to the parent cell.

similar molecule to the machinery outside the nucleus. This machinery consists of tiny particles called ribosomes, and all living cells are full of them. Using the information brought by the messenger molecules, they make what the cell needs in order to grow and function properly. The necessary raw materials are brought by transporters or carrier molecules, which are similar to the messengers.

These transporters and messengers, and also the chromosomes, are called nucleic acids, and these are of two types: DNA or deoxyribonucleic acid (the chromosome) and RNA or ribonucleic acid (the transporter and messenger). During the past twenty years, progress in molecular biology has been very rapid, and the discovery of the nature and function of DNA and RNA was of immense importance.

When the cell's requirements have been produced, they are sometimes packaged and exported from the cell – although this does not happen in bacteria. The place where the packaging occurs is known as the Golgi apparatus, after the scientist who first observed it.

Breathing without air

We breathe air so that it can be used in a chemical reaction to provide the energy we need to live or move, but bacteria are too small to breathe air as we do and are without lungs. They get their energy by breaking down certain chemicals in a way that releases energy in a form which they can use. This process of obtaining energy is known as 'respiration'.

Some bacteria need air to do this, others do not. In fact some bacteria can use air if it is there, but if it is not then they can convert themselves to living without it.

The virus

A simple virus can look like a crystal. It cannot move or grow and yet it is 'alive' in that it contains vital DNA or RNA and can reproduce using other cells' machinery.

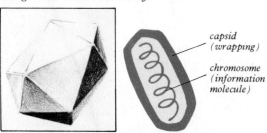

capsid
(*wrapping*)

chromosome
(*information
molecule*)

The enemies of bacteria

Most plants and animals – and not just humans! – contract various illnesses and diseases. Even bacteria sometimes get ill. This is when they are attacked by a member of that other group of tiny creatures called viruses.

The virus is so minute – at least 10 times and often as many as 500 times smaller than a bacterium – that it cannot generally be seen even with the most powerful optical microscope. Only the electron microscope has brought the virus within our field of knowledge and revealed its lack of complicated machinery. All it contains is one molecule of information (a chromosome) wrapped up in an outer coat of protective protein (a capsid). In some viruses, the capsid is in two parts, called the head and the tail.

The size and uncomplicated nature of the virus leaves open to debate the question as to whether or not it can truly be described as 'living'. Since, however, just about all it does is grow and multiply, it conforms to some extent with the definition of life with which we began.

The virus is a parasite, for it can only grow when it has attacked and entered another cell. Without any machinery of its own, it has to use the structure of another cell in order to reproduce itself. Viruses can attack any sort of cell, and they are usually harmful (or pathogenic). A lot of study has been made of the viruses that attack bacteria, and so we know most about this particular type. They are called bacteriophages – or simply phages – from the Greek words meaning 'baterium-eaters'.

Takeover in the factory

We have already seen how bacteria and other

The T4 virus is more complex.

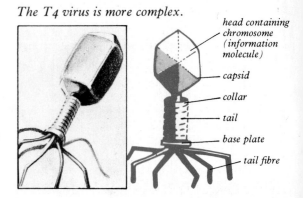

head containing
chromosome
(*information
molecule*)

capsid

collar

tail

base plate

tail fibre

The cell factory

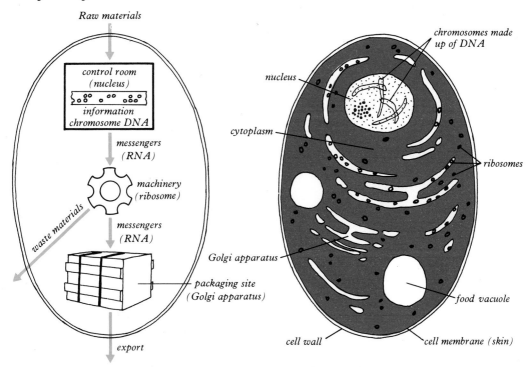

cells are rather like factories, with control rooms (nucleus), machinery (ribosomes), messengers and carriers (nucleic acids), energy sources, and so on. We have also noted that viruses lack any such machinery. This means that in order to multiply viruses must invade the bacterium factory, take it over and convert the machinery to their own ends.

The first problem is: how to break in? The more complicated viruses are made rather like syringes, with tails that can be squeezed up into a very tight concertina. When they have attached to the outside wall of a bacterium, they contract the tail and inject their information molecule into the cell.

Once inside, the virus's chromosome sends messengers to the bacterium's machinery with

The mumps virus seen through an electron microscope.

The common soil bacteria streptomyces-griseus, from which a powerful antibiotic has been made to fight disease.

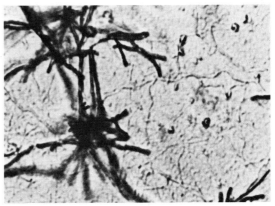

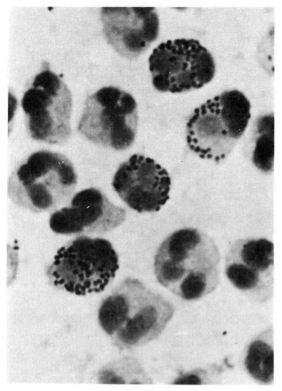

Pneumococci bacteria inside white cells.

different instructions. This stops the machinery making what the bacterium nucleus has ordered, and the ribosomes begin to obey commands from the information molecule of the virus. The factory has been taken over!

The machinery then makes hundreds of spare parts of viruses, which are soon assembled into whole viruses. Eventually the bacterium bursts apart and the new viruses are set free to go and attack another factory.

Some viruses do not multiply immediately after infecting the cell, but instead enter into a sort of partnership with the bacterium. They rest safely inside and multiply when the bacterium multiplies. This partnership is known as lysogeny. Viruses that do this are called 'temperate', whereas those that multiply immediately and cause the bacterium to burst are called 'virulent'.

You may be wondering where you could find such tiny creatures as bacteria or viruses. Well, believe it or not, they are just about everywhere! Bacteria live in the air, as high up as 18 miles/ 30 kilometres, and in the ocean, as far down as 6 miles/10 kilometres. We are constantly breathing them in, and there are countless millions of them on our skins, in our mouths, throats and stomachs. But before you go and have a bath to get rid of them, remember that many of them are good for you, especially the bacteria inside your stomach and intestine. These help you to digest your food properly, and are living inside you in partnership. You give them protection and food, and in return they aid your digestion.

But there are not only useful bacteria and viruses, there are useless ones as well. Some of these do damage and harm, and make people ill. This illustrates the fact that, though God made everything good originally, the world has been spoilt by sin and evil.

God is not going to allow his creation to remain like that for ever. He has already taken action to make a 'new heaven and a new earth' – ever since Jesus Christ came to take away the evil which has spoilt it all.

So even in these tiny things which are so small that we cannot see them, we can see the wonders of the world God has made – and which he is going to remake, perfect, more wonderfully still.

Take-over at the cell factory

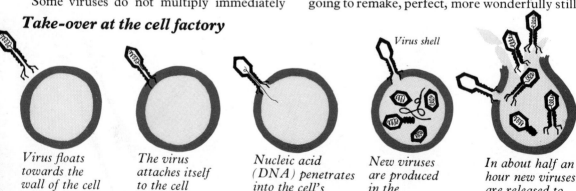

Virus floats towards the wall of the cell

The virus attaches itself to the cell

Nucleic acid (DNA) penetrates into the cell's cytoplasm

Virus shell

New viruses are produced in the host cell

In about half an hour new viruses are released to destroy more victims

The air we breathe

Colin A. Russell

**Many people once believed that the world
was composed of four basic elements –
earth, air, fire and water – which could not
be split into anything simpler. But we now
believe they were wrong, for none of the
four is a single substance. Water is a compound of hydrogen and oxygen. Air is a
mixture. There is a difference between the
two. A chemical compound never varies in
its make-up, but a mixture may contain
different substances in varying amounts.**

Pure air, unpolluted by motor cars or factory
chimneys, is a mixture of nitrogen and oxygen
(in a proportion of about 4 to 1), together with
a good many other gases such as water vapour,
carbon dioxide and a whole range of 'inert' or
inactive gases.

Oxygen

Of all these various components the really
important one for us is oxygen, even though it
accounts for only about 20 per cent of the
atmosphere. This is the gas which is essential to
life and combustion, or burning.

When we breathe, the air enters our lungs and
gives up its oxygen to the bloodstream. We get
our energy from a kind of combustion in our
bodies of the food we have eaten (or rather some
of it) and the oxygen is used in this process. So
we need a constant supply of fresh air, or the
oxygen will eventually be removed and all that is
left is the unbreathable residue.

Oxygen is also used whenever there is a fire.
It combines with the material that is burning to
produce oxides of whatever elements it con-
tained. Wood, for instance, yields mainly water
(hydrogen oxide) and carbon dioxide.

Now here is a remarkable fact. Although we
humans and most animals and fish breathe in
oxygen and breathe out carbon dioxide, the
opposite is true of many plants, at least in some
circumstances. They take in the carbon dioxide
from the air and give out oxygen. As a result of
this the oxygen level in the air remains almost
constant. It would be a strange coincidence if it
had happened quite by chance that these two
processes should exactly balance each other, so
that the vital oxygen should be present in
precisely the right amount for human survival.
That is just one of the reasons why I am com-
pelled to believe in a Creator.

Nitrogen

Important though it is, oxygen remains a minor
part of the air. It is nitrogen which tops the list
with over 75 per cent of the total. This gas is
remarkable for its lack of chemical reactivity. As
far as we are concerned as human beings, its
main role appears to be that of diluting the
oxygen – of calming it down, if you like. If we
were to breathe pure oxygen, as opposed to air,
we should soon be almost literally burned up.
Glowing embers will burst into flame if air is
replaced by oxygen, and we should certainly not
last long in an atmosphere of oxygen only. So,
except in certain medical cases, there is nothing
more suitable for us to breathe than ordinary
fresh air.

A flame cannot burn without oxygen. If a glass jar is fitted tightly over a lighted candle so that no air can seep in, the candle will use up all the oxygen and go out.

Although nitrogen gas is very unreactive and does not appear to play any direct part in the living processes of men and animals, this is not true for an important group of plants including clover and peas. These have within them certain micro-organisms which enable them to absorb nitrogen directly from the air. In this way, crops can be grown in places where the soil is poor in nitrogen, one of the necessary ingredients in a plant's diet. But these plants have another important role to play. By removing nitrogen from the atmosphere they help to compensate for another natural process – the fact that when plant and animal materials decay, their nitrogen is released into the air.

The two processes of gain and loss of nitrogen are delicately balanced so that the amount of nitrogen in the air at any given altitude hardly ever varies. Here is another example of the precision and balance which permits our kind of

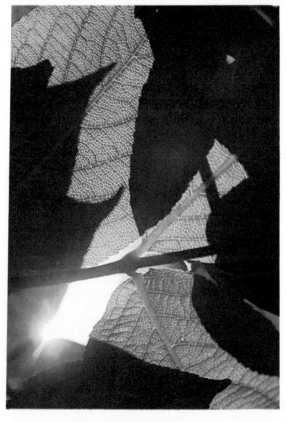

By giving out oxygen in the continuous process of photosynthesis green plants help balance the carbon dioxide and oxygen in our atmosphere.

life to continue and to thrive.

Oxygen and nitrogen together account for over 98 per cent of the air we breathe. Now we are going to look at two minor constituents which are much more important than you might suspect.

Carbon dioxide

One of the minor constituents of the atmosphere is carbon dioxide. For nearly 200 years we have known that this is the gas given out by animals as they breathe, and by fire, fermentation and several other natural processes. Again there are built-in means of controlling the concentration of this gas and preventing it from reaching too high a level. It has long been known that plants take it up as part of their process of photosynthesis – the creation of new material by plants, under the influence of light. Carbon dioxide becomes a building-block for the production of such complex substances as starch and sugars. The basic balancing act is quite simple: animals absorb oxygen and give out carbon dioxide, whereas plants absorb carbon dioxide and give out oxygen.

Nodules on a runner bean root contain nitrogen-fixing bacteria essential to the nitrogen cycle.

These remarkable plants are deadly insect traps. They grow in marshy conditions which are poor in the nitrogen they need for healthy growth. They have therefore developed an ingenious method of catching insects, dissolving them and absorbing the resulting rich 'soup' to supplement their diet.

The nitrogen cycle

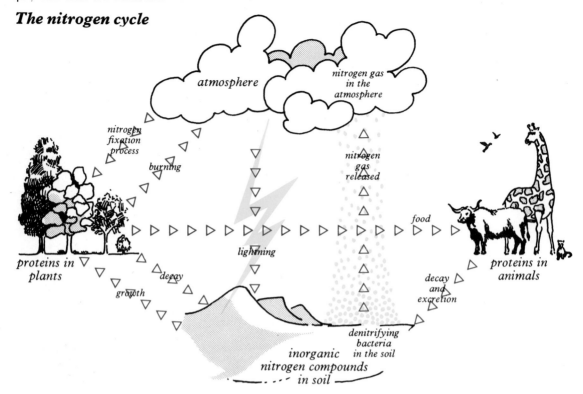

There is much more to it than this, of course. There are processes which remove carbon dioxide from the air (as when rain washes it into the sea), and yet others which restore it to the air. It sometimes issues from the ground, as it does in the famous Death Valleys in several parts of the world. In these the gas enters an enclosed valley and, since it is heavier than air, it tends to form a blanket over the ground in which no animal can survive.

The percentage of carbon dioxide in the air remains fairly constant, about 0·03 per cent So you might think that if it were doubled this would not make much difference.

In fact, however, we have now begun to realize how important the precise concentration is. Although the carbon dioxide in our atmosphere will let the sun's rays freely through, it tends to block the release of heat radiation from the earth. In other words it allows the earth to be heated up by the sun, but does not let it cool down quite so readily. This is called the 'greenhouse effect' because the carbon dioxide has a role similar to the part played by the glass of a greenhouse. As a result of this our earth has a warm atmosphere. But the more carbon dioxide there was, the greater this effect would be – and the hotter we

should get.

We have already mentioned the balancing mechanism by which the concentration of carbon dioxide is kept almost stationary. Almost, but not quite. It seems that over the last eighty years or so the balance of carbon dioxide in the atmosphere has been shifted ever so slightly. The cause of this change is man himself. During this period civilization's demands for energy have increased by an enormous amount, and nearly all the common sources of energy involve the production of carbon dioxide. Think of them. Every time you burn wood, charcoal or coal; every time you light a paraffin lamp or heater (or even a candle); every time a petrol or diesel engine bursts into life – in all these cases you are returning carbon dioxide into the air.

Of course we must not exaggerate this effect. All of this emission of carbon dioxide by combustion amounts to only about 1.3 per cent of nature's total, and in fifty years the increase is only about 30 parts per million. Nevertheless there has been a detectable increase in the average temperature over that period. So a slight change in our atmosphere could well cause a considerable change in our climates. This is certainly a case where man's large-scale alteration of the

The carbon cycle

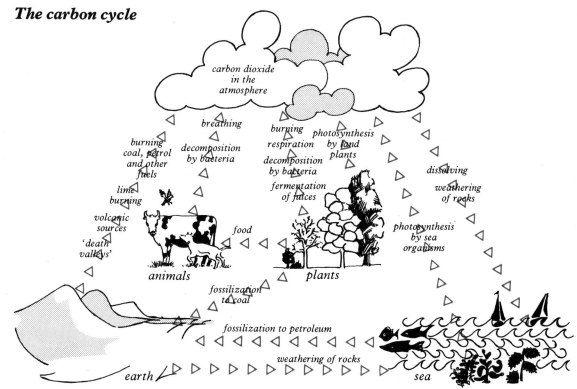

carbon dioxide
in the
atmosphere

breathing

burning

photosynthesis
by land
plants

burning
coal, petrol
and other
fuels

decomposition
by bacteria

respiration

decomposition
by bacteria

dissolving

weathering
of rocks

lime
burning

fermentation
of juices

volcanic
sources

food

photosynthesis
by sea
organisms

'death
valleys'

animals

plants

fossilization
to coal

fossilization to petroleum

weathering of rocks

earth

sea

environment God has given him could land him in serious trouble later on.

Ozone

One other very minor constituent of the atmosphere is the gas ozone. It is a near relation of ordinary oxygen, and indeed is made only of oxygen atoms. But whereas in ordinary oxygen the atoms go round in pairs (the molecule O_2), in ozone there are three together (O_3).

Some years ago ozone used to be a bit of a joke. It was supposed to be present in unusually high concentrations in the air of certain holiday resorts in Europe. It was alleged to have health-giving properties, and advertisements used the 'ozone' to try to persuade people to visit these resorts.

We know now that there is no high concentration of ozone in these places, and that in any case ozone is poisonous! If you have ever stood near a dynamo or electric motor and noticed the peculiar smell when it was working you may have detected small quantities of ozone, for it is formed by the passage of electricity through ordinary oxygen.

Apart from this, it is not found at ordinary altitudes – where the air has a remarkably

constant composition all over the world – to any extent at all. But if you go very high up, the composition does begin to change, and the air becomes thinner.

If you were able to ascend to about 17 miles/ 28 kilometres you would then discover a high concentration of ozone. This ozone belt may be one of the important reasons for the blueness of the sky. But recent experiments, including some from high altitude rockets, have demonstrated another fact.

We know now that this ozone blanket around us is in fact vital to the existence of life below. For the ozone absorbs certain of the sun's radiations (the short-wave ultra-violet) that would be exceedingly harmful to all living creatures on earth. As these rays strike the ozone layer the ozone molecules absorb them and are transformed into ordinary oxygen (two of O_3 giving three of O_2).

In this way the ozone forms a barrier between ourselves and the deadly rays from the sun. Until recently we had no idea about this, but it must always have been there. It is one of the many protecting devices provided by the Creator for the preservation of life on this most favoured planet.

Fungi and the food we eat

Barbara Drake

Every year more than 165 million pounds of mushrooms are broiled, sautéed, stuffed, cut up in sauces or sliced raw in salads in the United States alone.

But did you know that not only mushrooms but yeasts, moulds and other members of the strange kingdom of fungi are of major importance to our food, health, and very existence in the world?

Mushrooms are a valuable source of vitamins, minerals and proteins. But a whole pound of mushrooms contains only 90 calories. That is why so many are eaten by people watching their weight!

The mushroom

The mushroom as we know it is in fact only part of the plant, the 'fruiting body'. The main part, the 'mycelium' remains under ground. It is a mass of delicate grey threads, rather like an old man's beard. These threads, or 'hyphae', are a kind of 'root' but they are very different from the roots of an ordinary plant. Under a microscope we can see that these threads are made up of single cells, joined end to end. Each cell has a very thin cellulose wall enclosing the cell substance or protoplasm, and one or more nuclei.

At a certain time of the year these hyphae mass together and form a white egg-shaped body. This develops quickly and breaks open, revealing the new pink gills on the underside of the cap. This is the mushroom we know, the one that ends up as a tasty trimming to an appetizing meal.

This part of the mushroom is called a fruiting body because between each gill on the underside of its cap are millions of tiny seeds called 'spores'. These spores are minute and very, very light. But if any one of these ripe spores can reach open ground, it is capable of growing into another fungus plant.

In order to make this possible the mushroom has a special mechanism – a 'spore-gun' – which shoots the spores out from between the gills. The tiny spore is attached to the gill. A drop of fluid exudes at the end of a little stalk called the 'hilum'. Then the wall between the gill and the spore parts and the spore is shot horizontally about 0.1mm. The weight of the drop of fluid then makes it fall. The fluid evaporates and the spore is blown away by the wind. It settles on open ground, and a new plant begins to grow.

Which ones can we eat?

Not all fungi are good to eat, and you cannot tell the good ones simply by looking at them. In China they eat an ugly, dark-brown, ear-shaped mushroom. In some South Pacific islands they eat ochre-coloured 'witches butter'. Many of the mushrooms we call 'toadstools', which are considered inedible because they look peculiar, are in fact perfectly all right to eat. (But never try them yourself without asking someone who knows a lot about mushrooms.)

From a spore to a mushroom

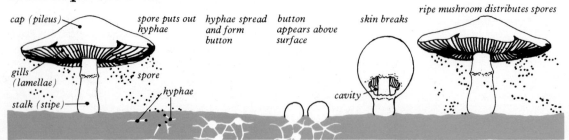

cap (pileus)   spore puts out hyphae   hyphae spread and form button   button appears above surface   skin breaks   *ripe mushroom distributes spores*

gills (lamellae)   spore   hyphae   cavity

stalk (stipe)

The beautiful but deadly Amanita Muscaria.

A mature giant puff-ball. The cracks on the surface are for the release of the spores inside the ball.

Taste and smell are not much of a guide either. Different mushrooms have all kinds of funny smells. Some smell like soap, others like radishes, the chlorine of swimming-pools, cod-liver oil, bitter almonds or rotten fish. Some smell good – others smell dreadful! Fungi have different tastes, too. Sulphur polyporus tastes of chicken. Others taste of oysters, kidneys or peppers. A Frenchman has written a report on mushrooms describing the flavour of 245 different kinds!

One mushroom which is good to eat and especially tasty is the morel, or spring mushroom. It has a spongy, pitted cap which varies in colour from tan to a rich brown and it is shaped like a pine cone. It is rarely found, as it appears in one place for only two weeks at a time, and we have not yet learned how to grow it.

Another delicacy is the huge puffball, which grows on rotten logs and in open fields. Unlike the morel, puffballs come up in the same place year after year. They can be eaten in all kinds of ways, and an imaginative cook can prepare puffball steaks, breaded puffball cutlets, mashed and creamed purée of puffball, or raw, sliced puffball salad.

Sulphur polyporus (the mushroom that tastes like chicken), grows on the sides of trees or dead logs in a row of fan-shaped orange or yellow shelves. It can be fried or stewed.

Another edible fungus is the shaggymane.

The cap resembles a guardsman's hat, white with brownish tufts sticking out. However, if it is not gathered at the right time it will dissolve into an inky black fluid.

Beware of this one

One mushroom you must beware of is the Amanita. Although it looks so beautiful, it can be highly poisonous. Some kinds are a soft delicate green, while others are bright red, spotted with white dots, or a cheerful orange, or creamy off-white. One is known as the 'Angel of Death', another the 'Death Cap'. The symptoms of Amanita poisoning occur some ten or twelve hours after the meal. The victim gets violent cramps, is sick, has convulsions and an intense thirst.

Hunting truffles – with pigs!

You may have eaten chocolate truffles, but did you know that there are fungus truffles? These are a great delicacy, and are very expensive indeed to buy. They cannot be seen above the ground, as they grow several inches down. Only their scent gives them away. So trained dogs – and pigs too – are taken out on 'truffle-hunts'.

The pig is the favourite hunter, as he has a

Colourful fungi

1. Wood fungus growing from a dead log.
2. Red cup fungi, generally found in damp ground or decaying wood.
3. Earthstar. As it grows it splits open to release the spores, making a star shape.
4. Fly amanita button, which is poisonous. The large cup at the base of the plant is called a volva.
5. Sulphur polypore, an edible fungus that tastes like chicken.
6. Amethyst Claveria, a coral-like fungus to be found from mid-summer to late autumn.
7. Scarlet cup fungi.
8. White morel. All species of this genus are edible and highly prized for their flavour.

powerful snout to root the truffles out, as well as a keen sense of smell to find them. In the past, people held very strange beliefs about truffles – that the mushrooms were formed when the thunder roared; or that they grew out of witches' spit!

Bread, wine and cheese

Nice as they are, mushrooms are much less important to our diet than some of the other fungi. What is it that changes a heavy lump of dough into a light, fluffy loaf of bread? What makes the juice pressed from grapes change into wine? How does a chunk of milk cheese change into blue gorganzola? In every case, a fungus has been at work.

The fungus we add to dough to make it rise is the yeast plant. This plant is so small that we can only see it properly under a microscope. It is made of a single cell, and grows by producing another cell on its side, like a bud. The new cell then either breaks off, or remains attached to the mother cell, starting a chain of daughter cells.

Yeast plants need sugar and warmth in order to reproduce themselves. In doing so they release energy and give off carbon dioxide. So when we add yeast to dough and leave it in a warm place, the yeast breaks down the sugar in the dough, and forms gas which makes the bread rise. Of course the yeast plants are killed by the heat when the bread is baked!

'Unleavened' bread, made without yeast, is thin and flat. It is eaten by Jewish families at Passover time, when they remember how God brought his people out of slavery in Egypt. On

The thin root-like hairs of a fungus are called hyphae. The black dots visible here are the sporangia containing spores.

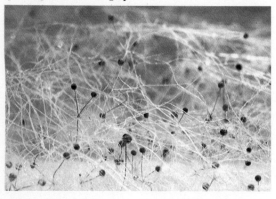

The gills of a mushroom

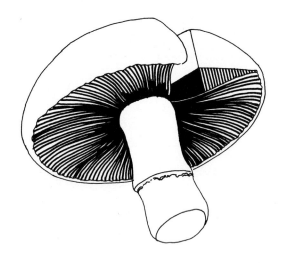

one gill (much enlarged)

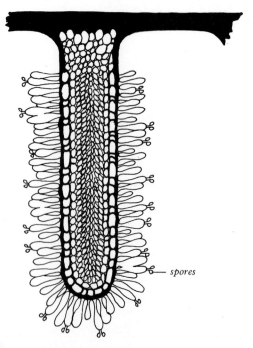

— spores

the night of their escape there was no time to wait for bread to rise!

Yeasts are found in the skins of many fruits, including the grape. It is these grape yeasts which break down the sugar to alcohol in grape juice, converting it into wine. In countries where drinking-water is often contaminated, wine may be the only safe drink.

Moulds are responsible for the special texture and flavour of many cheeses. White milk cheese is inoculated with a special mould which produces masses of blue-green spores in veins and pockets all through the cheese. The result is a 'blue cheese'.

'Manna' – a kind of fungus?

Fungi have been written about in many old manuscripts. The Bible records a specially interesting occurrence. In Exodus, the second book of the Old Testament, we read how God supplied the nation of Israel with food and drink during their years of desert-wandering. It was a long lesson in trust. God gave them 'manna' to eat. When the dew evaporated every morning the manna lay on the ground, fine as hoar-frost.

It is possible that the substance they gathered was a combination of an alga with a certain kind of fungus – lichen – which can absorb moisture from the air when there is none in the soil, and so survive in the desert. Lichen can be ground into flour and baked. It produces a bread high in protein.

This does not make the manna ('bread from heaven') any less wonderful. God, who made every kind of fungus, gave his people this special food, day after day, to keep them strong and healthy.

What do the fungi live on?

Wolves, deer, wildcats, goats, squirrels, rats, bears, hares, pigs and dogs – as well as human beings – enjoy eating fungi. So do many kinds of insects. But what do the fungi live on?

Unlike green plants, fungi have no green pigment, or chlorophyll. Without this, a plant cannot make the sugars, starches, celluloses, proteins and fats it needs for food. So fungi have to live on other plants or animals.

Most fungi – the 'saprophytes' – live on dead animal or plant material. Some – the 'parasites' – live on or in living plants or animals. Some are so well adapted that they can live on either.

Fungi even consume one another! One kind of mould will eat the bread made by the yeast fungus. Rot and mildew, signs of the presence of fungi, attack mushrooms. All sorts of food are quickly taken over by moulds which make them unfit to eat.

Fungi will also attack lifeless objects. When paint changes colour and peels off the walls of houses it may not be due to the weather, but to minute paint-eating fungi. When plastic buckets and other articles crack it may not be because of age or ill-treatment, but because fungi have eaten away some essential ingredients.

Vital to life

If all this sounds unpleasant, stop and think a minute. Could we really do without fungi? Not only do they give us food, they also break down all kinds of plant and animal remains, providing rich nourishment for the soil. Instead of dead material turning our world into a smelly rubbish dump, the fungi recycle it. They provide the essential nutrients for the life and growth of the green plant – and all life depends on that.

Only now is man learning not to waste things, but to use them again, to recycle them, to make them into something different for another use. We cannot afford to waste the precious things which God has designed for the world.

God has also given to man the job of looking after the world. He designed fungi to prevent waste, and to avoid pollution. Man must learn from him. We must learn to value living things. We must learn to use the earth's resources wisely, not selfishly grab them and throw them away when they are worn out. We need not only to look after the world God has made, but to learn from it as well.

A species of lichen, Ramalina calicaris.

Making things strong

Malcolm B. Waldron

When we want to make something for a special purpose, we choose our material with care. We make a knife out of hard steel, not soft lead or copper. We wrap food in foil that we can fold and that doesn't spring back.

Have you ever thought why some things are strong and tough, while others are hard and brittle; why some things stretch; why some things are springy? What is it that makes things strong?

What do we mean by 'strong'? When we say something is strong, we mean that it needs a lot of force to stretch it or bend it by a given amount. We need to be strong ourselves to do it, unless it is very thin. We all know from experience, for example, that it takes much more strength to

How metals bend

Each atom is resting on three others. They are held together by forces acting like invisible springs.

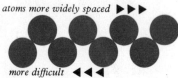

forces of attraction

When a metal is bent one layer of atoms slides an atom at a time over another.

Atoms are arranged differently in different metals. This means that some can be moved more easily than others.

atom planes closely packed ▶▶▶

easy movement ◀◀◀

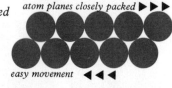

atoms more widely spaced ▶▶▶

more difficult ◀◀◀

Metals have to be tough but flexible for a building job like a suspension bridge. This is the famous Sydney harbour bridge, seen from underneath.

bend a steel tent peg than an aluminium one. You can think of plenty of other examples.

Hollows, humps and springs

Scientists have tackled this question by studying the very fine structure of metals, using X-rays, to find out how the atoms are arranged. Then they have used powerful microscopes to see what happens when these metals are bent or stretched. They have found that metals are made up of layers of atoms, rather like marbles in a bottle, with each marble resting naturally in the hollow made by three others underneath it. There are several different ways in which atoms can be arranged, some packed more closely than others.

When a metal is bent, one layer of atoms slides over the humps between their set of hollows, except that the atoms go over the humps one at a time, rather like the movement of a caterpillar! This takes much less effort than moving all the atoms at the same time. It is like a series of small rubber balls being rolled across a sheet of corrugated cardboard used to separate eggs or fruit.

In addition to the effort needed to make one atom move over the hump into the next hollow, there is also a force holding the atoms together, rather like invisible springs. The two things together determine the over-all strength of the piece of metal formed by the layers of atoms.

Weak or strong?

To come back to our two tent pegs: the thing that determines the strength of a metal is the way in which the atoms are arranged – the size of the hollows and humps, and the force that joins the atoms together.

In the great wisdom of God this has been worked out exactly right, so that we have metals suitable for every kind of purpose and as different from each other as lead, aluminium, iron or titanium (the new metal used in rockets and supersonic aircraft).

The same – but different

You may also have noticed some forms of a particular metal – iron, for example – are much stronger than others. Compare the blade of a good sword with a cheap spanner used for your bicycle. There are similar differences in strength between different aluminium alloys, and between copper and brass.

The reason for this difference is that small amounts of a different metal – different atoms of different size – have been mixed with the original metal atoms and prevent them moving smoothly over each other because they are no longer even. You could compare it with getting grit into a ball-bearing in your roller skates or a

Metals have to be heated to high temperatures to be mixed into an alloy. Here the molten alloy is poured out of a furnace, glowing red hot.

bicycle wheel, except that in this case it is done deliberately. Sometimes the atoms form new arrangements which behave more like chocks put under the wheels of a large truck or trailer.

Trial and error

Down through the centuries, man has found out by trial and error how to make alloys by adding one metal to another to get the properties he needs. He may find metal naturally, like alluvial gold in the rivers, iron in meteorites, or copper or tin in some shallow mines. He may refine metals by treating the compounds in which they occur as ores with heat and chemicals.

Until the last 50 or 100 years he did not understand very clearly why some things made metals stronger or more useful. Nowadays the metallurgist is a scientist who uses many scientific and technical tools to discover the reason for this. It is possible to find answers to our questions because our world has been created in a rational, orderly and consistent way. We can establish general rules. We can say, for example, that most things get bigger when they

are heated and that they change to a liquid at the melting temperature. If these things were not basically consistent and predictable, science as we know it would not exist. In fact it was Christian teaching about the way things have been made that formed the basis for the work of the first scientists. God made things in an orderly way. And he made man to look after them and be in control of them.

Strong – and beautiful

So far we have talked about strength only in relation to metals – which include silver and gold and platinum, things which are useful as well as beautiful. But there are other strong materials.

One of the most interesting of natural materials is the diamond. How beautiful diamonds are even before they are cut and polished. The transparent material allows the light to shine through it and the crystal faces that occur naturally cause the light to glint beautifully. The diamond has been formed as a crystal very slowly, deep in the earth, as it cooled down under immense pressure. Skilful cutting of the facets by a jeweller makes it glitter and sparkle with incredible shafts of light, all colours of the rainbow.

Nowadays, diamonds are not only used to decorate rings and crowns and make fine jewelry. They are also used in industry to cut the hardest substances to incredibly accurate dimensions, or to give teeth to the drills that bore down into mines or oil wells through the toughest rocks.

Diamond is the hardest substance known, even today, and although we can now produce small diamonds artificially by use of special equipment that works at high temperatures and extreme pressures, we still rely on finding the best diamonds just where they were formed.

What makes diamonds so hard?

Chemically diamond is the same as soot or pencil lead (graphite) or coal. In some parts of

The natural diamond is found in the rock where it was formed and is a clear irregular crystal. When skilfully cut each plane reflects light and colour and the diamond appears to sparkle.

The arrangement of atoms

Both diamonds and pencil lead (graphite) are made of pure carbon. It is the different arrangement of atoms within them that makes the difference between the two.

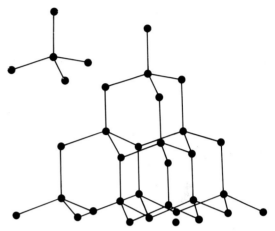

In diamond, each carbon atom is joined by four equally spaced bonds (forces of attraction represented by a straight line in the diagram) to other atoms. The whole structure is closely held together. The resulting shape makes the diamond very hard indeed.

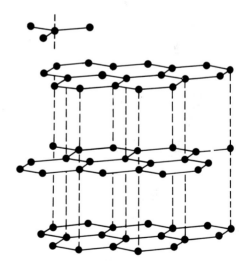

In graphite, the carbon atoms are arranged in flat sheets which are too far apart to hold a strong attraction. In the sheets each atom is attached by strong bonds to three other atoms as well as weaker bonds to atoms in adjoining sheets. Thus each sheet can easily be slid away from the others, leaving a mark on paper.

Preventing cracks

The tip of a crack under an electron microscope.

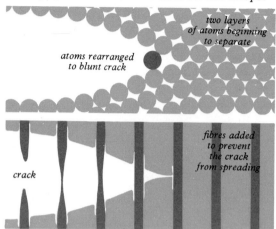

two layers
of atoms beginning
to separate

atoms rearranged
to blunt crack

fibres added
to prevent
the crack
from spreading

crack

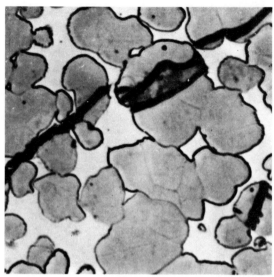

Under the electron microscope : a crack through the carbide grains in cemented tungsten carbide.

the earth's crust, where the temperatures and pressures have been less in the distant past, the same element – carbon – makes coal instead of diamond. Yet to look at, and in their uses, there is all the difference in the world between the two. Once again, the difference is in how the atoms are arranged.

The same atoms which are arranged in hexagonal plates in graphite, are arranged in a three-dimensional triangular structure in the diamond. The first structure allows the plates to slide easily over each other, leaving a black mark whenever they touch something. The second structure is completely different. It is absolutely rigid and has no point of weakness. That is why it is so hard that it will scratch or cut anything else. Virtually nothing will cut or mark a diamond except other pieces of diamond.

An interesting man-made material is boron nitride, which combines boron and nitrogen, elements lying either side of carbon in the regular arrangement of the elements from hydrogen through to uranium. The normal form is just like graphite, and has the same arrangements of atoms. The high pressure form is like diamond, but not quite so hard and strong.

Brittle or tough?

It is not just how hard things are to bend, or stretch, or cut, that makes us decide how strong they are. Glass can have a fantastically sharp cutting edge, but will break into dozens of pieces if it is dropped a short distance on to a hard floor. What is the difference between something that is brittle and something that is tough?

It is a very good thing that materials vary. Imagine what it would be like if all materials were tough! Our forefathers would never have been able to make sharp tools out of flints by chipping away at them. On the other hand, if everything were brittle, they would not have been able to use bow and arrows, bend branches over to make a house, fashion a sword or spear, or protect themselves with armour.

Hidden cracks

The thing that determines brittleness is the behaviour of countless little flaws or cracks which are found inside nearly all materials, possibly only a few hundred atom spaces long. The tip of the crack, if you could see it under a very powerful electron microscope, may just be the sharp point where two layers of atoms are beginning to separate, or it may be blunted by the atoms at the tip rearranging themselves to round it off.

A sharp tip means that the crack will open up rapidly when a force is applied to it, and the material will be brittle. In a less brittle material, the rounding crack will slow down or stop – so the crack will not spread across the piece.

Toughs for weaklings

Some materials that have sharp cracks and are

basically brittle can be toughened up by introducing into the basic atomic arrangement some small particles or fibres which block and divert the crack and so prevent it spreading rapidly.

Tungsten carbide is one very hard material which is used instead of diamond for cutting highly alloyed materials in a lathe, or boring through rocks. It is also very brittle and would shatter into pieces, but a small quantity of a metal (usually cobalt) is added to prevent cracks developing. This makes the cemented carbide tough as well as hard.

A variety of these composite materials is being used for modern advances in technology. Carbon fibres – which are very stiff and strong – are used to reinforce a plastic space filler and so produce a very light but enormously rigid material. This is being used in the building of the Concorde and will be used increasingly in supersonic and other aircraft. Even if the fibres crack, the soft plastic blunts the crack and holds it together.

Another more common example is fibreglass, which is used for car bodies, boats and dinghies, and many other things. In this material, glass fibres – again very strong and stiff – are combined with plastic. This provides a material which is much cheaper than one which contains carbon fibres but which has similar properties.

It is interesting to compare a modern composite with wood – nature's most prolific wonder material – under a microscope. In both cases the strong cell walls surround material with different properties. Under a powerful microscope, the broken surface of a fibre composite looks remarkably like a broken piece of wood. The modern material is in many ways a carefully contrived replica of something done in nature long before we even began to think of using materials as tools.

Nature's catapults

One other interesting thing about many materials is the fact that they are elastic. We mean by this that they will stretch or bend but immediately return to their original shape when the force is removed. It is not just elastic bands that behave like this. Most materials are 'springy', up to a point. However, the most common examples are made from rubber, the natural product of the 'rubber tree'. Rubber is specially treated to develop its elasticity to the full. But the secret of its behaviour lies in its molecular structure. Large strings of atoms are joined in a cross-linked net, often in a coiled spring-like form, so that the forces drawing the molecules to each other pull the material back to its original shape.

Even though many modern plastic materials have been developed for all sorts of purposes, the elasticity of natural rubber is still hard to beat. It still makes the best balloons, catapults, and some more technical things such as pressure diaphragms and so on.

The astronomer, Kepler, as he studied the motion of the planets round the sun, used to say: 'I am thinking God's thoughts after him.' This is true of every branch of science. In the development of new materials in our modern world we are following in the footsteps of God, the great Creator. He has not only designed different types of material in the world. He has also given to man the ability to develop them and control them and to be able to create as well, using the raw materials God has given us.

In making composite materials we often copy nature's originals.

The fibres of natural wood.

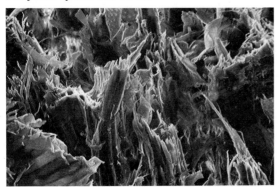

The fibres of a modern composite.

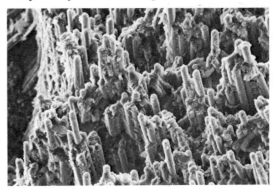

The dust that brings life

F. Nigel Hepper

If you suffer from hay fever, you will know about pollen. It is the minute grains of dust produced by flowering plants. What is it for?

Flowers must usually be pollinated before their seeds can form. Pollen is carried by the wind, by insects and even by birds. But flowers have all sorts of other strange, ingenious ways of getting their pollen to other flowers . . .

Pollen seems very insignificant blowing about in the summer wind. But it has a very important function. In fact the closer you examine the world about us, the more amazing God's work of creation appears. Not only has everything a

A bee drinking the nectar from a flower, with his long hollow tongue.

place and purpose, but it is beautifully and individually adapted. Each part is vitally related to the other parts: it does not matter how small and insignificant it may seem.

Watch a bee flying from flower to flower. His hairy body is covered with yellow dust – pollen from the flower stamens. Do you know that he is helping with a very important part of the plant's life-cycle?

Flowers contain young seeds, or female ovules.

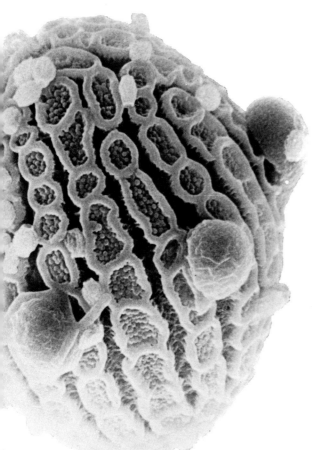

One pollen grain, seen under the electron microscope. Each flower's pollen has a different pattern.

To enable them to develop into seeds in the fruit, the ovules have to be joined with (or fertilized by) the male 'seed' from another flower. The pollen is the male 'seed'.

This vital link is brought about in many different ways, some of them very ingenious. We can only marvel at them. But one of the simplest is wind.

Being so small and light, pollen grains from the hazel catkins, for example, are blown about by the wind and some of them land on the female stigmas which are in separate flowers.

The date palm actually has separate male and female trees: pollen must be blown by the wind from one to another. Even in ancient times the Babylonian people apparently understood this, for they used to cut the branches of pollen-bearing male flowers and hang or shake them among the female trees in case the wind did not do it for them.

Equipped for pollen gathering

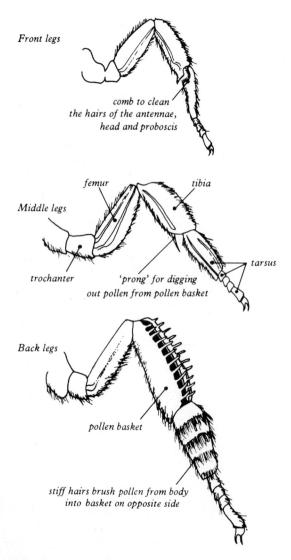

Front legs

comb to clean
the hairs of the antennae,
head and proboscis

femur   tibia

Middle legs

trochanter   'prong' for digging
out pollen from pollen basket   tarsus

Back legs

pollen basket

stiff hairs brush pollen from body
into basket on opposite side

A bee has six legs, three on each side. Each pair has a special job to do in the business of pollen gathering.

Bees with long tongues

We have all seen insects, especially bees, visiting flowers. The honey bee is really a 'domestic animal': we can keep it just like any farm animal. We take its honey in exchange for the sugar which is placed in the hives. But it does another important job when it makes the honey from the nectar it collects. If the hives are placed in an orchard, the thousands of bees hurry from flower to flower pollinating them as they go, and this in turn ensures that the fruits develop.

The bumble bee, although it lives wild in small colonies and not in hives, is also very important. When European red clover was grown in New Zealand, it was discovered that the seeds were not being 'set', for the flowers were not pollinated, although there were plenty of hive bees there. It was not until European bumble bees were also taken to New Zealand that the clover seeds developed.

This was because the nectar in the clover flower is too deep down for the short tongue of the honey bee to reach, so they were not interested in visiting the flowers. But the bumble bee has a long tongue with which it can reach the nectar, and so it pollinated the flowers as it went round.

Favourite colours and scents

Bees are attracted to flowers by their colour. Experiments have been done to find out which colours bees can see. They cannot see red, for example, but they can see colours that we cannot see, such as ultra-violet. Some flowers reflect ultra-violet light which attracts the bees, although we see quite a different colour on the petals. Blues and yellows are particularly attractive to the honey bee. These can also attract a bee from quite a long distance away.

Fragrance can also play an important part in attracting insects over shorter distances. Night-flowering plants are often white and show up in the dark, but they also have a very strong fragrance which attracts the night-flying moths to the flowers. Some butterflies are also attracted by the scent, but most of them rely on flower colour, and fly in daylight.

Some flowers, on the other hand, have a smell like decaying meat! They are carefully designed to attract flies that live on meat. Remarkably, these flowers are often a dark crimson colour, like flesh with dried up blood. So flies are tricked into visiting the flowers, and even lay their eggs on them, pollinating the flowers at the same time.

Tricks and traps

Plants often lay traps to attract visitors. The bee orchid, for example, has flowers that look very like a female bumble bee. When the males visit the flowers and try to mate the supposed

A fleabane flower.

The same flower, photographed by ultra-violet light. This is the colour the bee sees.

A bumble-bee pollinating a flower

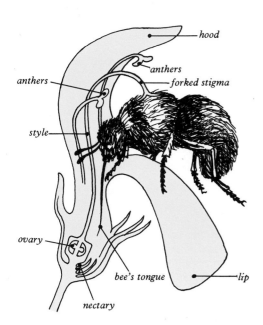

hood

anthers

anthers

forked stigma

style

ovary

bee's tongue

lip

nectary

Before the bee reaches the nectar the stigma touches its body and collects pollen already present. As it penetrates further into the flower the anthers strike its back and deposit pollen which the bee will carry to the stigma of another flower.

A honey bee feeding on a fleabane.

female, they pollinate the flowers as they move from one to the other, apparently not realizing their mistake.

Orchids have two small bags of pollen called pollinia in each flower. When a bee visits the flower to try to reach the nectar his head touches something that releases the pollinia, which then stick to his head with a special sticky disc at the end of a short stalk. As the bee flies off to another flower the stalk bends over so that in half a minute the pollinium is in just the right place for it to be inserted into the female 'stigma'.

Some flowers even trap small insects. The wild arum, sometimes called Lords and Ladies, has a large upright flower near the ground which gives off a nasty smell. This attracts small insects and, when they land on it, their feet slip on little drops of oil that cover part of the flower, and they fall into the cup at the bottom. Of course they try to crawl out, but they are prevented from doing so by downward pointing hairs.

In the cup at the bottom of the flower there is food for them, in the form of a kind of nectar. The next day the insects are showered with pollen from the stamens above so that, when the hairs at the entrance to the cup wither, the insects, now covered with pollen, can crawl out and fly away, only to be attracted to another arum flower near by. Once more they are caught and, in trying to escape, rub the pollen off on the female stigmas.

An even more elaborate trap method is used by the Bolivian plant Aristolochia, a kind of Dutchman's Pipe. A series of windows or thin parts of the otherwise dark trap cause the insects

Aristolochia, found in Bolivia. Its elaborate trap is set to catch insects and dust them with pollen. They may then escape and fly on to the next plant.

to crawl towards the light to find a way to escape. In fact they are just being lured towards the stamens, where they get dusted with pollen and carry it away to another flower when they do eventually escape.

The wasp and the fig

For a long time it was known that the finest Smyrna fig-trees would not develop edible fruit unless bunches of the useless uneatable figs called caprifigs were gathered and hung among the branches. The reason for this was a mystery. We now know that it is due to a marvellous sequence of events.

This fig is pollinated by certain chalcid wasps now called fig wasps. These insects are entirely dependent for their complicated life-cycle on the inedible male caprifigs which the tree bears three times a year, in winter, summer and

The sycomore fig-tree.

Many insects and animals help in the pollination process, including butterflies, beetles and humming-birds.

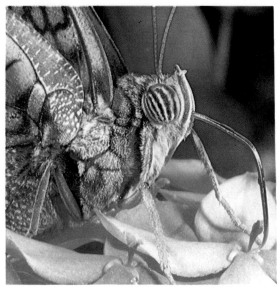

autumn. They lay their eggs in them, the male and female hatching at just the right time, and the female wasp flying out to find the next growth of caprifigs which has developed at the right time. In their search for a place to lay their eggs they pollinate the female fig and clean edible fruits develop. When the Smyrna fig was taken to America no fruits were obtained until these insects were imported too. (Our usual cultivated fig, however, develops its fruits without the aid of any insects.)

Timing is important, too, in the pollination of the sycomore fig – the one mentioned in the Bible when Zacchaeus climbed a sycomore-tree to see Jesus. The eggs laid by the female wasp inside the fig take just five weeks to develop into mature insects, which is the same length of time the fruits need, too. Then the males hatch first and, after mating with the females as they come out of their tiny flowers, they bore through the upper part of the ripe fig. However, the hole made by the males is not for their use since they do not have wings. But it is a means of escape for the females who squeeze through, taking with them loads of pollen they have carefully packed into special pockets on their legs! They carry the pollen dust to another young fig where they lay their own eggs.

Birds, bats and bushbabies

In the American continent the famous humming-birds are very important pollinators. These brightly-coloured birds are very small and can hover in front of a flower, sucking up the liquid nectar with their long tongues. For the bird to stay in mid-air it has to beat its wings about 3,300 times every minute. The flowers are also brilliantly coloured, often bright red, to attract the birds, as the birds' sense of smell is poorly developed. The humming-birds dart from flower to flower, getting dusted with pollen from the stamens that are long and hang far out of the flowers.

Some flowers are pollinated by bats. These 'flying mice' have to land on the flowers and put their heads inside to reach the nectar. In the process they get themselves covered with pollen.

In East Africa in 1954, two zoologists found that a group of bushbabies known as the thick-tailed galagos visited the baobab trees on eight consecutive nights. They fed on the newly-opened flowers, moving from one to another, burying their faces in them. When the flowers fell the next day each showed signs of having been licked and chewed and the small fleshy sepals almost completely eaten. By the light of a torch on subsequent nights the zoologists could see a pale ring around each bushbaby's face where the pollen dusted the fur. Although the animals were feeding on the flowers, they were eating only the outer parts. The seed-producing parts of the flowers remained undamaged.

God's design

Next time you watch a bee visiting a flower, think about the job it is doing. Each one of these methods of pollination, and thousands more, are so carefully planned and accurately timed that we are left amazed by the sheer variety and richness of God's world.

So what seems to us to be just dust is vital to God's creation. And it is carried about in ways which make us marvel at his care for the world he has made.

Sun, wind and rain

Timothy J. Stevenson

Next time you are feeling grumpy, try this. Find a nice open space out of doors, run round in a large circle three times, stamp your foot and shout 'I command you to rain.' You will be obeyed.

Mind you, you will have to be rather patient. It will probably take years. Of course there will be rain sooner than that, but that doesn't count because it would have come anyway. There will come a rainy day, however, which would not have been rainy if you had not run round in that circle and shouted. To see how such a strange thing can be true we must find out something about how the weather works.

We live on the outside of a great big ball of assorted solid stuff – or you could say a tiny speck of solid stuff, it all depends what you are comparing it with. About two-thirds of this

earth is covered with water. Around the whole thing is a thin layer of gas that we call the atmosphere, the air. The various goings-on in this gas are what we call weather.

The great stirrer

Apart from one thing, that would be the end of the description of planet earth – a dead and useless place. That thing is the sun, which stirs the atmosphere into movement by its rays of light and heat. Parts of the earth near the equator get much more than their fair share of heat, while the parts near the North and South Poles get much less. Now if you heat air up it expands, that is it pushes outwards and grows thinner and lighter. In the same way cold air squashes together and gets heavier. Because

Where the wind comes from

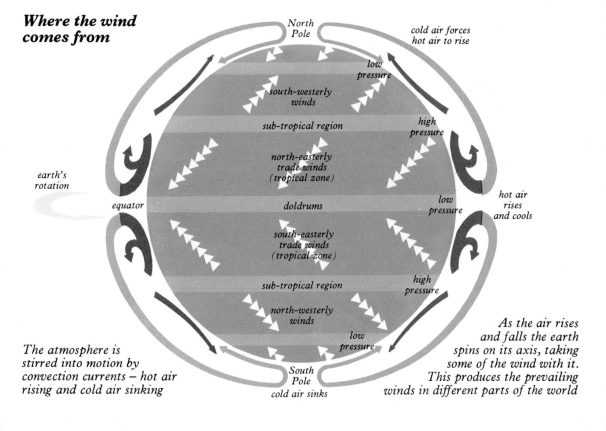

The atmosphere is stirred into motion by convection currents – hot air rising and cold air sinking

As the air rises and falls the earth spins on its axis, taking some of the wind with it. This produces the prevailing winds in different parts of the world

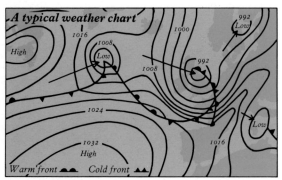

A typical weather chart

Low marks the areas of depression. The arrows show the direction in which they are travelling. High marks an area of anticyclone or high pressure. The lines, called isobars, join up the points which have the same pressure.

Photographs from space are now being used for more accurate weather prediction. Large areas of the earth can be shown at once and cloud movements plotted.

Even cloud formations over the east coast of America, taken from 100 miles up.

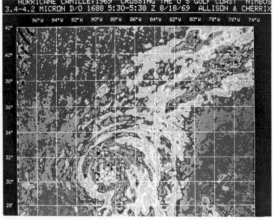

A colour-coded picture of hurricane Camille.

it is lighter, hot air tries to float upwards. Heavier cold air sinks downwards. This is why smoke is blown upwards from a fire. It is why, if you open a refrigerator door, you can feel cold air pouring over your feet.

Air is heated up at the equator and rises. It then tries to flow round the earth to the Poles. Once there, it cools down and sinks towards the ground. To complete the circle the air has to flow back to the equator. The picture shows this sort of simple flow, which we call convection. Convection is also one of the ways in which a fire spreads warmth through a room.

The spinning earth

This idea of the sun's heat driving air from the equator to the Poles and back is too simple. It leaves out the fact that the earth is spinning round. Of course the air goes round with it. As the earth spins, places on the equator go round on a journey of 24,900 miles every day, at a speed greater than a thousand miles per hour. On the other hand, places near the Poles have a much smaller circle to go round. That means they are moving much more slowly.

Now what happens when air from the equator tries to blow north? It gets into the same sort of trouble you might have if you jumped off something rapidly spinning round. As it moves north it passes over ground which is spinning less fast than it is. So it changes from a south wind to a south west wind. (A south wind is one that comes from the south, so that it is actually going northwards.) The name for this strange happening is the Coriolis effect.

Whirlpools of air

The fact that winds can never go in the direction you would expect is very important. It is part of the reason for the great swirling patterns you see on the weather charts. The simple convection from equator to Poles and back is twisted into complicated and ever-changing flows of air. One common arrangement is a depression. There is one in the middle of the weather-chart shown here. A depression is an area of low pressure – the air is slightly less squashed up than usual. You would expect this low pressure to suck in air from outside and, poof! – no more depression. The Coriolis effect stops this happening. Instead of flowing inwards, the air finds itself flowing round and round the low pressure area, not

How conditions affect the weather

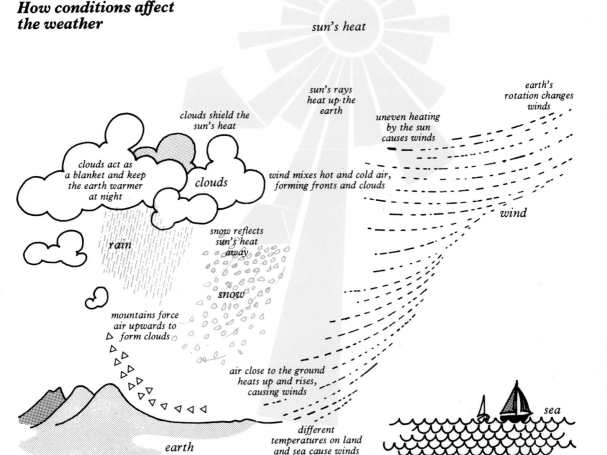

sun's heat

sun's rays heat up the earth

earth's rotation changes winds

clouds shield the sun's heat

uneven heating by the sun causes winds

clouds act as a blanket and keep the earth warmer at night

clouds

wind mixes hot and cold air, forming fronts and clouds

wind

rain

snow reflects sun's heat away

snow

mountains force air upwards to form clouds

air close to the ground heats up and rises, causing winds

sea

earth

different temperatures on land and sea cause winds

---

filling it up at all quickly. The same thing can happen with high pressure, which is called an anti-cyclone.

Pity the poor weatherman

It is becoming clear that forecasting the weather is not very easy. There are many things that make the job even more difficult. The sun can heat up land quite quickly, and the land heats the air over it. The sea is quite different, it takes weeks to warm up. The expanding and contracting of the air over land as it is heated by the sun and then cools at night changes the patterns of the wind.

In a long hot period the air near the ground can be heated much hotter than the air high above. This means that it is lighter than the air above it. The whole atmosphere wants to turn upside down! The result can be the violent storms that often end a spell of hot weather.

The water carriers

By far the most important thing that all these movements of air do is to carry water vapour about. Water vapour is quite invisible. It is a gas. Look carefully at a boiling kettle. Near the spout the vapour coming out is quite clear. A little further away a white cloud of 'steam' forms. This is made up of very many small drops of water. (The word steam is also sometimes used for the clear water vapour, just to be confusing!) On a dry day, the cloud does not blow away as smoke would, it just disappears.

What happens is this. Water vapour cannot be squashed up too much or it turns back to water. The colder it is, the more easily it turns to water. As the vapour comes out of a kettle, two things happen. It spreads out in the air, but it also gets colder. At first the getting colder is more important and drops of water form. When the steam has spread out a bit more, the opposite can happen and the droplets dry away to nothing. Only clear water vapour is left in the air.

Clouds are formed by the cooling of air that is full of water vapour. Often this happens because some air has gone upwards for some reason. Air gets colder as it goes up and gets thinner. (It gets thinner as it goes up because there is less air on top of it squashing it down. It gets colder because the air molecules lose some of their energy as they spread out.) Often the getting cooler wins over the thinning out, and drops of water are formed. Sometimes it is not drops of water but crystals of ice. If the drops grow big enough to fall to the gound without drying away, rain falls.

Many things can cause wet air to be forced upwards and form clouds. The heating up of the air near the ground by the sun can do it, and so can mountains when wind blows over them. It can also happen when the large-scale air movements try to mix hot and cold air. The hotter air is lighter and flows up over the colder air, often raining down its water on the way. This is called a front.

No mere passenger

Water is not just carried about by the winds, it changes them. One way it does so is quite obvious when you think about it. Clouds shield the sun's heat from the earth, making it cooler. This, in turn, affects the air temperature and pressure. If

Different cloud formations caused by the prevailing wind conditions.
High cloud ceiling.

A dramatic flash of lightning.

it snows, then much of the sun's heat is reflected back to space instead of heating the earth and air. On a slower time-scale, rain can change things by causing plants to grow. These in turn make differences in what happens to the sun's heat, and in whether future rain flows away or is held to dry off into the atmosphere again. Everything affects everything else.

Water vapour works for its living in the atmosphere in another way. A lot of heat is needed to turn water into vapour. (You may have noticed that it takes much longer to boil a saucepan of water dry than it does to bring it to the

Cirro-stratus.

circle change the weather – even if he does stamp and give high-sounding orders?

Many things act together in the atmosphere: wind, water, heating by the sun, clouds, land and sea. Each obeys its own, often complicated, rules. Most important, each can alter what the others do. It is a fact about things which are complicated in this sort of way that small changes grow into bigger and bigger changes. Suppose that by magic you could arrange the atmosphere *exactly* as it was a month ago. Pressure, temperature, winds, clouds, they would all have to be just right. Conditions on the ground and at sea would need to be correct too. If you could do this, then this month's weather would be just like last month's. You could not afford to make the slightest mistake, though. A mistake would not show much on the first day, but would begin to make differences on the second and third. The differences between this month and last would grow and grow, so that in the end the weather would be quite different. Even so small a thing as someone running can stir the air and set off changes that grow really big if you wait long enough.

Human beings are not capable of that kind of 'magic' though. The nearest thing we can get to it is by making a computer pretend to be the atmosphere. A computer can 'act out' weather much faster than it really happens. If you start it off with the weather as it is now, it can work out how the weather will change. The trouble is that it has just the same problems you had with your magic! However good it is, if it starts out with a slightly wrong picture of today's weather, the errors will grow and grow. For this reason exact weather forecasting will probably never be

boil.) This heat is given back when liquid water is formed again. In the atmosphere some of this heat can be turned into energy, causing violent storms. We have seen that air high in the atmosphere is cold, and rising air naturally cools down as it expands. The forming of clouds slows down the cooling of the air and helps to keep it warm and light, which encourages it to rise even more. The results can be as dramatic as a tornado.

What about that running?

Now let's go back to the point where we began. How on earth can someone running round in a

Mackerel sky.

Cumulo-nimbus.

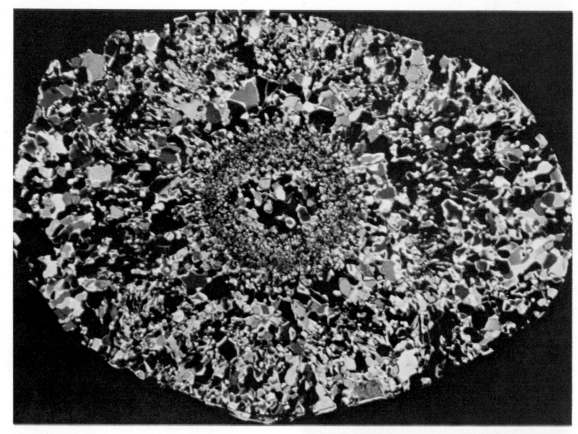

A cross-section of a hailstone under polarized light. It is made up of layers of tiny crystals of opaque ice and larger crystals of clear ice.

When rain comes through such cold air that it freezes, the result is a hail storm. Hailstones can be nearly as big as tennis balls, but are usually about 5 mm across.

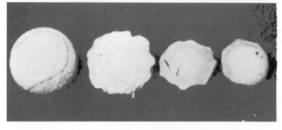

possible for more than a week or so ahead. Longer range forecasts can be made by looking up the records to find a year which started off much like this one; you then say that this year will carry on as that one did. This is useful, but it can never be very exact.

The world of people is every bit as complicated as the weather. There are millions of us, each affecting what others do and think. A tiny act of kindness may make someone else more cheerful. He may do his job better, help other people, avoid angry scenes. This will make small differences to the people round him, and so it will spread out. Given time, the whole world will be slightly different because of that first kind act. Nothing we do is too small to matter.

Animals that 'see' with their ears

George S. Cansdale

The tiny bats that spend the night in the air hunting for insects are remarkable animals in many ways. They are the only furred animals that really fly, and though they do not make such long journeys they are more expert in the air than almost any bird.

The scientific name for bat means 'animal with hand-wings'. If you examine one carefully you will see that each wing has a framework like a hand with long thin fingers. The whole is covered with skin that you can almost see through. This construction makes the wing very flexible, so a bat can change direction instantly – which birds cannot do so well.

How a bat hunts in the dark

Some night animals have wonderfully effective eyes that open up wider and wider as it gets dark. Cats are like this, and so are owls, which can hunt easily when we humans can't see a thing. In fact, scientists now tell us that our

A colony of bats in a cave, Tamana, Trinidad.

eyes need about three hundred times more light for us to see our way around than an owl needs to find its living.

But bats have tiny eyes. So how do they manage to find and catch insects in the dark? If you look closely at some of the insect-eating bats you will notice that their ears are large and movable, and sometimes a very complicated shape. Hearing is obviously more important to bats than seeing. This clue set scientists on the road to finding out how bats can see in the dark.

They kept some in a laboratory to study their habits over a long period. The first problem was getting them to feed, for they are used to catching all their food in flight. This means that flying insects are the only food they recognize. These little bats had to be taught to accept live insects offered one by one in the fingers. Then they were set to travel over a kind of obstacle course, consisting of a number of poles and ropes hanging from the ceiling. First, without hurting the bats in any way, scientists covered their eyes with sticky tape. It made not the slightest difference. They flew around and between the poles, even though they sometimes

bat hears echo

sound bounces off object

sound pulses sent out by bat

How a bat uses echo-location

A bat in flight, showing the hand-wings adapted from the long fingers and webbed skin of the forelegs. The bat hunts the moth by hearing, not by sight.

had partly to fold their wings to get through. It was obvious that these bats did not depend on their eyes at night.

Built-in echo-sounders

Next, the research team unbandaged the bats' eyes, and instead put tiny plugs in their ears – with immediate and striking effect. The bats were almost helpless in the air, hitting the first pole they came to and falling to the ground. As soon as the plugs were removed the bats

were flying again as confidently as ever.

Quite clearly they were using their ears. Yet bats make comparatively few sounds that we can hear, certainly not enough to give them all the information they need to fly around so accurately and catch all their food. Even the bats'

An Eagle Owl needs good vision to hunt at night, so his eyes are large and sharp.

ordinary little calls are too high for some people to hear at all, so the next step was to set up special apparatus to listen in to the different sound vibrations made by the bats. They were far beyond anything that the sharpest human ear could pick up. Only electronics made this research possible.

When the apparatus for measuring the vibrations was switched on, it was found that the bats were sending out a stream of tiny pulses or sounds which bounced off objects and came back to the bats. This principle is called echo-location, or finding direction by listening to echoes. A fraction of a second after the bat sends out a signal it receives an echo back. It not only hears this echo but it can interpret and understand it in terms of distance and direction. Even more important, it can act on this information quickly enough to fly through a most complicated obstacle course, or catch an insect in the air.

Not only can a bat tell where an object is, it can decide what it is at the same time. If a stone is thrown in front of a flying bat it will probably turn towards it to check it. But long before it reaches the stone it will have found out that it is not good to eat, so it turns away and leaves it. A bat's senses are in some ways more accurate than the latest and most expensive radar systems that man has invented. In fact radar and sonar, its equivalent under water, were developed as a result of learning how animals

The long-eared bat uses his ears in echo-location. His eyes are very small and weak.

Why we cannot hear a bat's voice

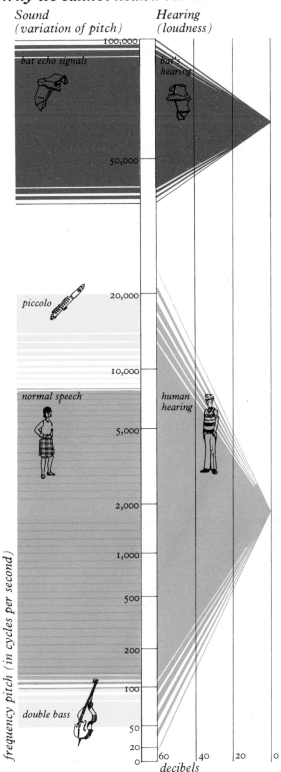

Sound (variation of pitch)

Hearing (loudness)

bat echo signals

bat's hearing

100,000

50,000

piccolo — 20,000

10,000

normal speech — human hearing

5,000

2,000

1,000

500

200

100

double bass — 50

20

frequency pitch (in cycles per second)

60   40   20   0

decibels

A sonar device in use in an oil rig in Canada as a depth meter.

like the bat use echoes. We still have much to learn from the world God has made!

How dolphins learn their tricks

We have only recently discovered that the same methods of echo-location used by the bat are also used under water by the dolphins.

Some scientists used to claim that no animals could make or hear sounds under water – simply because they themselves could hear nothing there! But to hear under-water sound an animal needs special under-water ears that can pick up vibrations passing through water. Human ears are designed for sound waves passing through air, so they are useless for this.

A special receiver called a hydrophone was made which picks up these sounds, turns them into an electric current and, with a complicated bit of apparatus, shows them as patterns on a screen, or transforms them into a range that our ears can receive. As soon as a hydrophone is lowered into the water, we find that the sea is full

Depth measurement by deep-sea sonar

Time between send-out and return of signal is registered on a micro-second clock

Time shown × speed of sound = depth of water

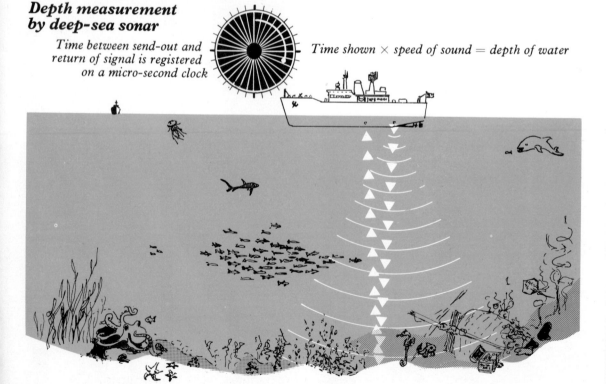

Dolphins leaping high out of the water Although they are air-breathing mammals they are perfectly adapted to water and are powerful and graceful swimmers.

of all sorts of noises. Many kinds of marine animals and fish can make sounds, though we do not know how all of them are made or what they are used for. Certainly some of them are used in echo-location, and this is true of the dolphins.

Dolphins live mostly in the Atlantic and Pacific oceans, though one or two species live in fresh water. The smallest are under 2 metres long, the largest maybe 3 or 4 metres, and they feed entirely on fish and other fairly big water animals.

Although they are shaped like fish for maximum efficiency in travelling through water, they belong to a completely separate group of animals. A basic difference is that they are warm-blooded and breathe air. This means that they must put their noses above the surface at least every few minutes to breathe out and then in again. They are perfectly suited for their life in the sea and their echo-location system is just as sensitive as the bat's. Some dolphins do well in zoos, where they are taught to do interesting exercises.

One of these exercises shows how echo-location works.

A dolphin comes to the edge of the pool and the trainer puts a little cap over each eye. Then he throws several floating rings into the water, just the right size for the dolphin to collect on its pointed nose. On command it swims around, quickly finds the rings and returns them to the trainer, who rewards it with a fish.

Like the bat, the dolphin has senses so accurate that it knows just what is sending back echoes, so even if the water is muddy it can find fish and avoid the rocks. Sometimes it swims very deep, far below where light can reach, and echo-location is just as effective there too.

Both bats and dolphins are equipped with this highly complex system of location as part of their adaptation to their environment. Only now are we beginning to learn some of their secrets, and putting them to use for ourselves.

Pips, hooks, parachutes and gliders

F. Nigel Hepper

When a squirrel hides hazel nuts or acorns in the ground, he is providing himself with a store of food for the winter. But he is doing something else, too. He is helping to disperse the seeds from which new trees can develop.

The dispersal of seeds is a vital part of the life-cycle of plants, and it takes place in an amazing variety of ways. The seeds are always in the fruit, although the fruit of plants and trees may be as hard as nails, or soft and juicy and good to eat. We can plant the seeds – the 'pips' of apples and oranges for example – and watch the new trees beginning to grow.

Many different kinds of animals, as well as wind and water, have a part to play in scattering or dispersing the seeds. Sometimes the whole fruit is dispersed; sometimes the seeds are separated from the fruit, which remains on the parent plant, and dispersed on their own.

By fur and feather

Every gardener knows that birds like to eat berries! Usually it is the bright colour of the fruit that attracts them. They eat the juicy pulp, but they also swallow the pips and berries – and so they play an important part in seed dispersal. The seeds are shed in their droppings, perhaps miles from where the fruit grew. In West Africa there is a vulture which disperses the seeds of the oil palm. Vultures normally live on flesh, but this particular one has taken a fancy to the palm's oily fruits which have some of the characteristics of meat.

Bats also help in the process of seed dispersion. Most places in the tropics have their colonies of fruit bats – large, chattering creatures that hang all over a particular tree near a village during the day. At dusk they fly away to the nearest fruit plantation where they rob the trees of the fruits, carry them away to their roost and scatter the seeds. The bats are attracted not by bright colour, as they fly at night and in any case are colour-blind, but by the smell which is often strong (and to us not very pleasant).

Other mammals, as well as bats, can be seed distributors. In Southern Africa a rather large mammal called the aardvark or ant-bear burrows into the dry soil to eat the fruit of a kind of cucumber. The seeds pass through it and are left in its dung near its burrow, where they germinate. As the fruits grow underground nobody would know where they were if this animal did not find them and distribute the seeds.

You will have noticed how your pets get their fur tangled up with little burs. These are really fruits with tiny hooks on them. With a magnifying-glass or a low-power microscope you can easily see the little hooks on cleavers or burdock, for example. They are like miniature fish-hooks and do their job very well. Sometimes they stick to your socks or jersey. You and your pets are helping to disperse the seeds when you pick them off!

Even some insects, such as ants, are seed distributors. Certain seeds, especially of the pea family, have an oily gland attached to them. The ants like this oil and carry the seeds away to their nests. When the oil has gone the seeds are usually left unharmed to germinate. Harvester ants also store enormous quantities of grass seeds.

Not all seeds are dispersed by animals, though. Many are carried by wind or water. Some very small seeds, like those of orchids, as well as the spores of fungi and ferns, are carried high up into the air and blown for enormous distances. Most of them die because they fall in places where they cannot grow, but others manage to survive and develop into new plants.

Reaching the islands

Have you ever wondered how the seeds reach islands in the middle of the ocean? Biologists have wondered, too, and they have been watching to see what grows on new islands – for these

A dandelion head is made up of hundreds of nutlets, each with a feathery parachute attached.

do still occur! In August 1883, for example, there was an enormous explosion as the volcano blew up on the island of Krakatoa between Java and Sumatra in Indonesia. That island disappeared but a new one developed. In the last few years another volcanic island has appeared off the coast of Iceland in the North Atlantic. Both Krakatoa and the new Surtsey Island have been carefully watched.

Plants began to grow up on the sea shore. These must have come from seeds carried by the ocean currents. Even coconuts grew on Krakatoa, after being washed up by the waves. The great big fruit of the coconut has a buoyant fibrous layer which makes it float very well and the sea water cannot penetrate to the hard central nut.

Many other seeds that are able to float are killed by the salty water of the sea, so it is not every seed that will grow when it reaches an island.

Great tropical rivers bring fallen trees down to the sea and bits of wood which drift across to the islands. Sometimes trees like this carry seeds or even plants that are not killed by the salt water – and it need happen only once for most plants to become established on the island.

Islands are also visited by birds, and they carry seeds in their feathers, on their feet or inside their crops. The seeds on their feathers are often hooked on, like those that attach themselves to the fur of mammals. Water birds carry the seeds of water plants on their feet. Geese, for instance, fly from Greenland to North America, or from northern Russia to western Europe, to escape the worst of the winter. Then they fly back to breed. Each time they go they

Methods of seed dispersal

By wind
1. The milkweed has a delicate parachute.
2. The lime-tree fruit has a 'wing' to help it glide.
By water
3. The coconut floats away from its parent tree.
Birds
*4. Shiny blackberries look tasty enough to catch
the eye of any bird.*

4

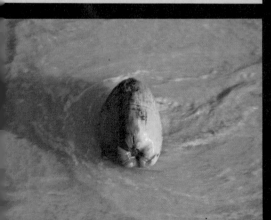

Explosion

5. *Laburnum pods twist and split open sharply.*

6. *Seed pods of the geranium uncoil like springs to scatter the seeds.*

7. *The round end-caps of these moss spore capsules fly off like miniature fireworks.*

8. *The boat-shaped pericarps of a violet seed-pod explode, hurling the seeds away like a catapult.*

9. *The squirting cucumber, common in the Mediterranean region.*

Hooks

10. *These goose grass burs have attached themselves to someone's sock. When he pulls them off he will be helping with their dispersal.*

An experiment to show seed dispersal by ants

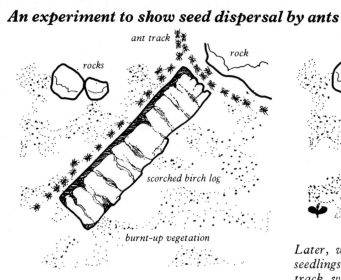

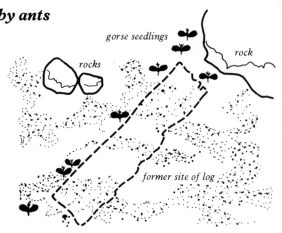

A few days after a heathland fire. All vegetation has been burnt in the area of an established ant track.

Later, when plants begin to grow again, gorse seedlings are already found growing along the ant track, where they have been dropped. This shows that ants have been responsible for dispersing the gorse seeds.

may carry seeds with them, and some plants are known to occur just where the geese go.

Gliders and jets

Some seeds are specially equipped for dispersal by wind. You will have seen the miniature parachutes – each carrying a tiny fruit – which float away when you blow a dandelion clock. The plumes of willow-herb and thistles, too, enable them to catch the wind and float away until they land and grow – often in somebody's garden, where they are not very welcome!

Many trees have fruits with 'wings' – the elm, for example, produces little discs with the seed in the middle. The winged fruits of the sycamore and the 'keys' of the ash really do whirl round like helicopter blades. Again they are specially designed for survival: the seeds themselves are quite heavy, and the height of the tree gives them a chance to land well away from the parent, with room to grow. Some tropical trees have seeds with very thin papery coats which float on the air like model gliders.

Not all wind-borne seeds rely on gliding. There are the jet-propelled seeds of the squirting cucumber, a common weed in the Mediterranean region. As the fruit ripens it begins to squeeze the seeds inside and there comes a time when it blows itself off its stalk and the seeds are shot out like bullets from a gun. The force of the 'explosion' is such that they are able to travel for quite a distance.

Many other plants have explosive fruits too. On a hot summer's day you may have heard the little cracking noise in a gorse bush caused by the pods splitting open. When the pod begins to dry there is such a strain on part of it that it suddenly explodes, twisting the sides apart and scattering the little peas in all directions. Balsam, or touch-me-not, has another explosive mechanism which throws the seeds when you touch the fleshy walls of the fruit. In the cranesbill and acanthus families there is even a tiny catapult for the seeds which are shot out of the fruit.

So in one way or another the seeds are scattered away from the parent plants to begin the cycle of growth all over again. They depend on all kinds of things for survival – their own special design, wind and water, birds and animals, even you and me. Look out for all the different seeds and fruits and try to decide how they are dispersed – you might get some surprises!

A drop in the ocean

Colin A. Russell

There is an old proverb which says that constant dripping will wear away a stone. And that is certainly true as far as water is concerned. Its power in nature is enormous, and so is its abundance.

You do not need to live near to Niagara falls to realize how much water there is on the earth. It is our most abundant liquid by far – billions of tons of it, in the oceans, in the atmosphere as water vapour and as clouds, and in the crust of the earth itself. Even our bodies are 64 per cent water, and some plants 90 per cent. We find it everywhere, even in tropical lands in drought – for without water there could be no life.

Chemical analysis

Because of its abundance, water has excited the attention of chemists for many hundreds of years. Until comparatively recently it was thought to be an element or single substance, something that could not be decomposed into anything simpler. Less than 150 years ago many were unsure about what it really was. However, at the end of the eighteenth century it had been discovered that water is formed when the gas hydrogen burns in air. Shortly after that it became clear that water is a compound, not an element, and consists of hydrogen and oxygen joined together in the proportion 1:8 by weight. As we would say today, two atoms of hydrogen are combined with one atom of oxygen, hence the most famous of all chemical formulae – H_2O.

A chemist always tries to examine any substance in its purest form. Impurities limit and distort his findings. So when we examine water in a chemistry laboratory we do not normally take it straight from the sea or a river, or even a tap. The water has to be purified first.

One time-honoured way of doing this is by distillation. Water is boiled, its vapour is condensed back to a liquid and the original impurities are left behind. The product is called 'distilled water'. But we are only imitating a natural process. The sun evaporates water from the sea, leaving the salts behind. The water vapour condenses when it cools and returns to the earth as rain or dew – the purest form of natural water. If you are used to drinking ordinary water, you would find that rain water and distilled water had a very flat and insipid sort of taste. There can hardly be a chemistry laboratory anywhere in the world that does not have its supply of distilled water.

Chemists, generally speaking, are not chiefly concerned with what we might call the large-scale effects of water in our environment – the part it plays in our weather, for instance. But they are interested in the characteristics (properties) of the pure material which can very

Structure of a water molecule – H_2O

A hydrogen atom by itself is in a highly reactive state because it has one electron.
The stable arrangement for a hydrogen atom is either none at all or two electrons outside the nucleus. For oxygen the preferred number is eight, although the oxygen atom itself has only six. By sharing electrons contributed by each atom, all the orbits are filled in the molecule water, which is thus very stable.

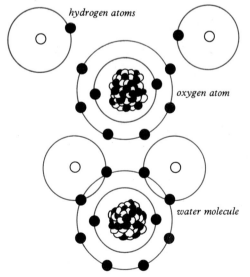

hydrogen atoms

oxygen atom

water molecule

often explain some of its big effects in nature.

We all know some of the simple properties of water. It freezes at 0°C and boils at 100°C. It is a colourless (except perhaps in very large quantities), almost tasteless, and odourless liquid. And of course it freezes to ice and boils away to water vapour or steam. But there are several ways in which water is a very remarkable liquid, and three in particular in which it is highly unusual.

Slow to heat – slow to cool

Water has a very high specific heat. That is to say, water can take, or absorb, a lot of heat without its temperature rising very much. A certain amount of heat will raise the temperature of the same weight of different substances to a varying extent. This is measured as the 'specific heat' of the substance concerned. For example, if you heat a kilo of mercury and a kilo of water for exactly the same time, with exactly the same source of heat, you will find that the temperature of the mercury is far higher at the end than the temperature of the water.

Water takes a longer time to heat up and to cool down than anything else. That is why you are more likely to burn your mouth with heated food that has a high water content!

The fact that water has the highest specific heat of any substance we know has important

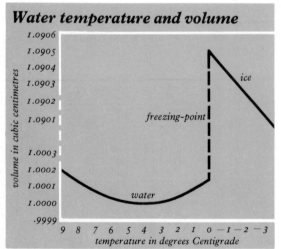

Water temperature and volume

volume in cubic centimetres

1.0906
1.0905
1.0904
1.0903
1.0902
1.0901

ice

freezing-point

1.0003
1.0002
1.0001
1.0000
.9999

water

9 8 7 6 5 4 3 2 1 0 −1 −2 −3
temperature in degrees Centigrade

This chart shows the change in volume of one gramme of water as it cools down. At first it contracts until it reaches 4°C, then it begins to expand. On freezing it expands much more to become ice, and the ice then contracts slowly as it gets colder.

Water in three states

steam

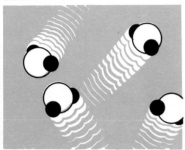

liquid

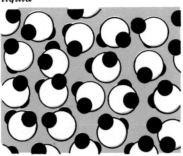

ice

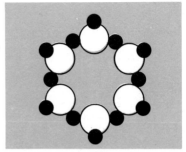

Water molecules in steam are widely spaced and dart about rapidly, colliding with one another.

In a liquid state the water molecules are closer together and slip easily over one another. They tend to associate with each other through forces of attraction called hydrogen bonds.

When frozen, water molecules may form into hollow rings. The ice has low density and will float in liquid water. Water molecules are now held rigidly in place by the hydrogen bonds.

consequences. It means, for example, that the oceans do not undergo rapid changes of temperature just because the air above them does. They heat up slowly and cool down slowly. This makes possible the survival of living things, which would be destroyed if the temperature rose and fell too quickly. Again, it means that we human beings can survive fairly drastic and rapid changes of external temperature, because our bodies (which have a high

Water in its three forms :
A gas: *water vapour rises high with the air and turns to steam above a hot geyser in New Zealand.*
A liquid: *the mighty Niagara Falls.*
A solid: *drifting ice-floes off the coast of Japan.*

water content) can accept extra heat without undue harm. A drink of cold water really does cool you down!

What happens when it freezes

Another unusual thing about water shows up when you cool it. Take almost any other liquid and cool it down gradually. As you do so it will contract; that is to say, a given weight will take up a smaller volume. As the temperature drops it will become more and more dense; its density (or specific gravity) increases as it gets colder. In most cases this happens right the way down to freezing-point. Now of all the thousands of liquids known to science only one or two do not show this behaviour, and one of them (by far the most important) is water.

As the temperature of water drops, the density increases in the usual way until it reaches $4°C$ above the freezing-point. Then, quite suddenly and unexpectedly, the density decreases and goes on decreasing until it reaches $0°$, when the water freezes and turns into ice. Almost alone among liquids, water has its maximum density not at freezing-point but a few degrees higher. Reverse the process, and allow the ice to melt. The density increases for another $3°$ or $4°$ and then decreases, as with every other liquid. But those first $4°$ are crucial. Imagine some water being cooled from (say) $3°$ to $0°$. The density now decreases so that the ice is slightly less dense than the surrounding water – therefore the ice floats on water. But this behaviour is extremely unusual. In nearly every other liquid

The fact that water freezes is vital to many life-processes. It can also take many beautiful forms.
Icicles among the berries.
Broken ice on a puddle.
Crystals of ice in a river.
Hoar-frost on ferns.

the solid form sinks. In other words, the usual behaviour is for a liquid to freeze from the bottom upwards, but water freezes from the top downwards.

Just imagine what would happen if this were not the case. The oceans as they froze would gradually turn into one solid mass of ice and this would mean that the chances of marine life surviving a winter would be reduced to almost nil. But as it is, there is a protecting ice-cap on top of the Arctic and Antarctic seas with water underneath that is quite warm enough to sustain the lives of fish and other sea creatures. So this peculiar property of water means that marine life has been able to continue despite severe drops of temperature in the air above.

There is something else that follows from this strange behaviour of freezing water. In northern Europe, where sub-freezing conditions occur every winter, water-pipes made of lead tend to burst during a frost. This is because the water expands so much on forming ice that the soft metal pipe is cracked. The effect does not show until the thaw sets in and the liquid water escapes through the crack. But the damage was actually done during the freezing process.

To the owners of lead water pipes this is a great nuisance. But the same kind of process takes place in the soil and in rocks when the temperature drops below zero, with good effects. Water in the ground expands and crumbles the soil, so making nourishment available to the plants and also making it easier to plough and dig. Similarly, the rocks are cracked, and much of the scenery in the temperate regions of the earth owes its shape to this kind of action in the distant past.

The universal solvent

Many centuries ago the predecessors of the modern chemist, the alchemists, had amongst several strange objectives that of finding the universal solvent: a liquid that would dissolve everything. They never discovered it. Yet in a sense the answer to their problem lay right to hand in that commonest of all liquids – water. For water has a most remarkable ability to dissolve a vast number of different things. Admittedly, in many cases it does not dissolve them to any great extent. Thus, although it dissolves glass, because the solubility of glass is so very small you can keep water in glass bottles. But it dissolves many other things.

Oxygen dissolved in the water sustains life in the seas. Carbon dioxide is also soluble to some extent in water, and that solution is responsible for much of the weathering of rocks made of limestone. Again our scenery is affected by this – but so also is our health. Water that has attacked limestone contains calcium which is essential to our diet, and especially for bone development in young children. Many other 'trace' elements – minute quantities which are essential to our diet – come to us in solution in water. No other liquid has quite the same power to dissolve such

a vast variety of chemical substances. It seems as near to a universal solvent as we are ever likely to get.

Why?

Why does water have these strange unexpected properties? It is possible to account for it at two levels. At the rather learned and technical level, we can say that one reason appears to lie in the existence of things called hydrogen bonds between water molecules. Within the last forty years chemists have come to know quite a lot about these. It seems that water is the best of all examples of a hydrogen-bonded liquid.

But at a deeper level we can say that the amazing behaviour of the one liquid that is so plentiful and so essential to life illustrates the planning of the Creator God who made the world and all that is in it. Life (as we understand the term) would be quite impossible without an abundant liquid like this that possesses not just one but all three of the special properties of water. As a twentieth-century chemist, and a Christian, I would accept both these explanations as valid.

Water in the solar system

Water in its three forms – ice, vapour and liquid – is only found in a relatively narrow ring between Venus and Mars. Closer to the sun it becomes only vapour. Further from the sun it turns to ice. The earth's orbit is in the middle of this ring, the best possible place for the life process as we know it

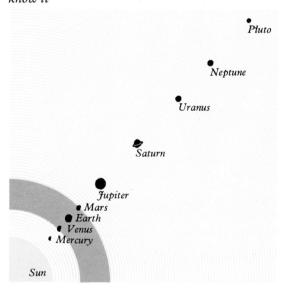

Pluto

Neptune

Uranus

Saturn

Jupiter
Mars
Earth
Venus
Mercury

Sun

Creatures of the sea-shore

Morag L. Ellison

Mention the sea-shore to most people and they think of sandcastles and sunbathing. But in fact this narrow strip between sea and land is one of the most fascinating parts of the whole created world.

Forget the wide, sandy beaches and head for the rocky areas. If you are prepared to look closely, beneath the stones and ledges, in the crevices and pools, you will find a strange and beautiful world – an ancient world, yet one where the struggle for survival and adjustment to varying conditions goes on continually. Indeed the sea-shore is so densely populated with such a variety of animal and plant life that it is perhaps the best place for the amateur naturalist to begin his training.

Variety of life

You will find many different species: sea anemones, shrimps and hermit crabs in the

If you look closely, you can pick out beadlet sea anemones, limpets, top shells and pink tufted Corallina weed in this pool.

pools – and even small fish; shore crabs and starfish will be hiding under the larger stones, while all sorts of worms can be found burrowing in the gravel between the rocks.

The most obvious form of plant life is, of course, seaweed. Green, brown or red, it may be over a yard long (like the oarweed) or just a tiny tuft of green 'cladophora'.

Beneath the forests of seaweed, a world is waiting to be discovered: snails, periwinkles and topshells; limpets clinging so firmly to the rock; barnacles and mussels even more permanently attached; or dog whelks moving freely about, prepared to hide away in the crevices only when the weather gets rough.

Perhaps the best place to look is in the dark, damp space beneath a ledge. Here the rocky walls and roof will be covered with sponges, hydroids, sea mats and sea squirts – often looking more like plants or pieces of rock than the creatures they really are. You will also find sea slugs here – among the most beautiful of shore animals – feeding on the sponges and hydroids.

These sea-shore creatures have essentially the same sort of problems as all other animals; how to cope with their particular environment – in

The common star fish on a sea lettuce.

this case, how to avoid being swept away every time the tide comes in; how to get food; and how to ensure the continuation of their species without creating a population explosion which would crowd them out of their chosen ledge or pool.

Holding on tight

Creatures that live on the sea-shore have to be able to survive both on dry land and under the water. They have to cope with two entirely different sets of living conditions.

Since there is absolutely nothing they can do to stop the tide from coming in twice a day, they must either find a burrow or crevice where they can hide away from the waves or learn to cling tightly to the rock surface. Part of the wonder of God's creation is the way these animals can survive such a dramatic and inevitable change in their environment.

Barnacles and mussels spend all their adult life cemented firmly to the rocks, and many other species which breed in colonies – the sponges and sea squirts, the sea mats and hydroids – survive by the same method. Some of the worms build their hard white tubes right onto the rocks, while even the sea anemone – though quite capable of moving about freely – prefers to cling on tight.

The search for food

Fixing themselves firmly to the rock surface

A hermit crab living in a cast-off whelk shell.

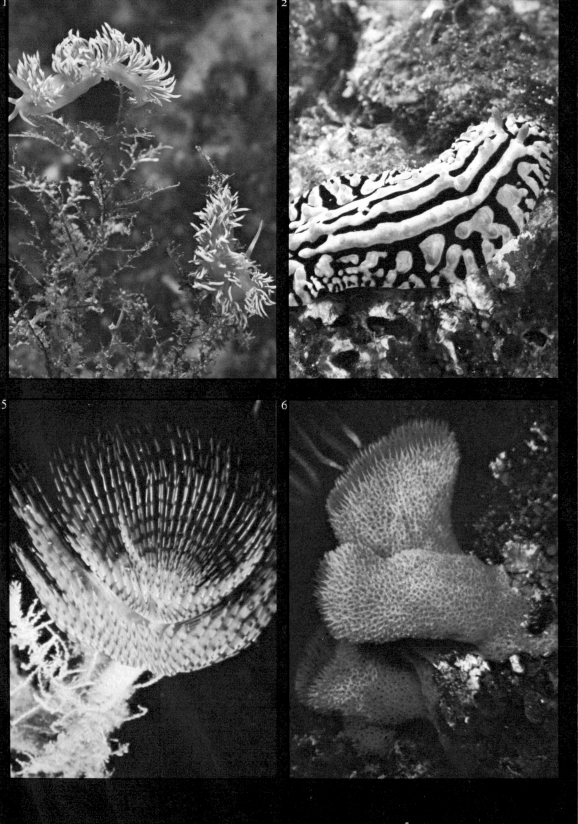

3

4

Colourful sea creatures

Slugs and worms do not usually look very beautiful, but sea slugs and worms are quite different.

1. A Nudibranch sea slug from the coral reefs of Mozambique. The tufty cerata on their backs contain stinging cells.

2. The startlingly patterned sea slug Phyllidia, also from Mozambique.

3. Hexabranchus adamsi swims by undulating its frilled edges.

4. Berthella granulata scavenges for food in the tide pools on the south coast of South Africa.

5. The peacock (fan) worm, Sabella pavonina. By waving its tentacles through the water the worm extracts minute particles to eat.

6. Callyspongia, a sponge which looks like a plant but is in fact an animal. It filters water through its tubular shape to catch plankton, which it digests.

7. Oaten pipes hydroids, Tubularia indivisa.

7

The sea anemone is found in shallow temperate and tropical waters. This picture shows the anemone with tentacles outspread, ready to catch its prey.

may have provided these animals with a secure home, but it also presents them with a fresh problem: how to find food when they cannot go foraging.

Like the animals of the wood or hedgerow, some shore creatures do, of course, browse around for food, searching through the seaweed, hunting and trapping their prey. But many species have been created with the ability to live entirely on whatever meals the tide brings to them, feeding on the microscopic water-borne plants and animals which make up the plankton.

Each species has its own particular method of catching the food it needs. Barnacles are constantly casting their 'nets' – a network of bristles arranged on their legs. Tube-worms enmesh the tiny planktonic creatures within a crown of minute tentacles projecting from the front of the tube. Sea anemones and hydroids catch the tiny animals individually by lasooing them with microscopic stinging threads on their tentacles.

Many other creatures which encrust the rocks – the sea squirt, for instance – suck in continuous streams and strain out particles of food as the water passes right through them. It is as if they were living in a soup from which they sift, strain or pluck their meals. And so

A beautiful trap

The sea anemone looks like a beautiful under-water flower but to its prey it is a deadly trap. Each tentacle is equipped with hundreds of stinging cells or cnidoblasts. Each one can whip out an enormously long filament and inflict a paralyzing sting on its prey. The tentacles then close in, moving the victim towards the anemone's central mouth.

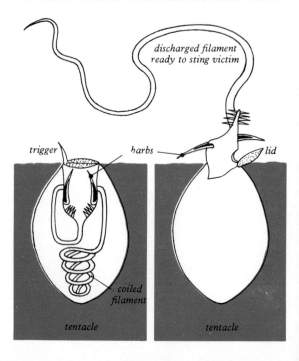

they can avoid the danger of being swept away, yet still get the food they need.

Room to live

All would seem to be well in this sea-shore world. The creatures have a secure home and a continual supply of food. But what happens when they reproduce? If all the young barnacles and mussels were to fix themselves firmly to the rock alongside their parents, there would soon be no room to spare, while other, more distant, rocks would remain empty.

Once again, it is all a matter of design. Just as the adult is perfectly fitted to its particular conditions of life, so too with the young.

Frequently the young not only look different from their parents, but also act very differently. They have special features which enable them to float or swim rather than stick to the rocks, with sense organs to help them find their way about and various devices to protect them during the risky time they spend as part of the plankton from which so many creatures snatch their food.

Growing up quickly

The young sea squirt, for instance, begins life floating with the rest of the plankton, enclosed in its tough egg case. As the single cell – the fertilized zygote – begins to divide, it quickly develops a muscular tail and a body with organs for sensing light and 'up and down' movement. In a few days the egg case breaks open and a little larva emerges, looking rather like a tadpole. It has no mouth, and at this stage does not feed at all. Its main business is to swim, to get up into the currents of the sea, and to drift away in search of a new place to settle. When it lands and sticks down, its tail disappears within a few minutes and it very quickly changes to the adult form. There it will remain for the rest of its life, feeding off the plankton from which it has emerged.

The young sea-urchin larva spends a much longer time floating in the plankton, and during this stage, it grows from the one cell in its jelly case to a hollow ball of cells actively swimming around. Soon its mouth develops, and for several weeks it feeds on smaller planktonic plants and animals. As it gets larger, it sprouts long spiky arms. These help it to float – like the feathers of a shuttlecock – and make it difficult for other creatures to eat it.

Barnacles and one limpet hold on tight to the rocks.
At low tide they are exposed to the air and close up tight.

Under water they open up and feed by trapping tiny plankton in their 'nets' of delicate tentacles.

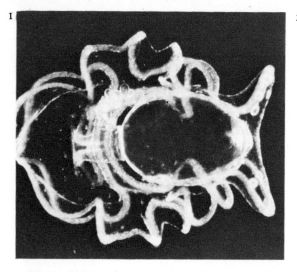

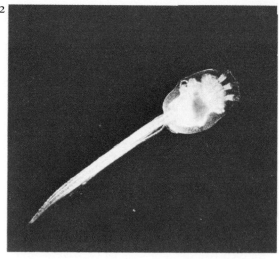

Worm larvae also spend some time in the plankton and so need to be protected from predators. In addition to the long spikes or

bristles which they grow, they are often almost transparent so that other creatures cannot see them very easily. They look quite unlike the

Development of a sea-urchin egg

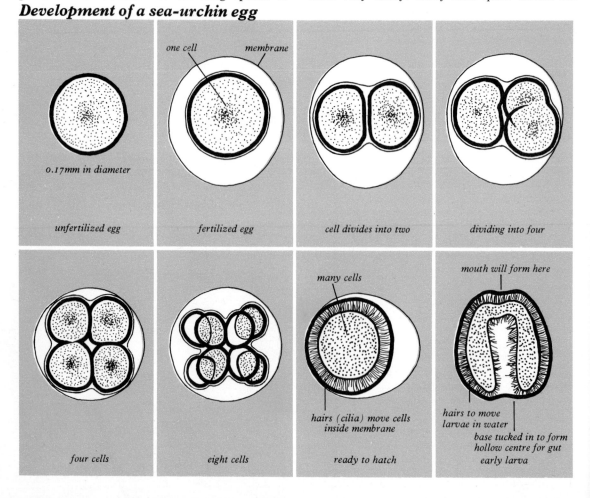

0.17mm in diameter	one cell membrane		
unfertilized egg	*fertilized egg*	*cell divides into two*	*dividing into four*

		many cells	mouth will form here
four cells	*eight cells*	*hairs (cilia) move cells inside membrane* *ready to hatch*	*hairs to move larvae in water* *base tucked in to form hollow centre for gut* *early larva*

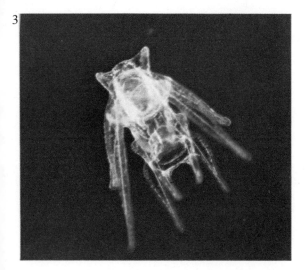

3

Often the larvae of sea creatures are quite different from the adults. They are very small and their life is full of danger, as they form part of the plankton which many other species, including the gigantic whale, use for food.

1. Auricularia larva of sea cucumber.

2. Ascidian larva of sea squirt.

3. Echinopluteus, sea urchin larva.

long, thin worms that we find on the shore but, as they grow, the more familiar segments appear one by one, and soon they drop out of the surface currents to burrow into the sand or build their tubes on the rocks.

But one creature – the young barnacle – has to change very rapidly to the adult form. While swimming and feeding in the plankton, it goes through several stages – shedding its hard outer 'skin' or exoskeleton as it grows too large for each successive covering. The final larval stage – the 'cypris' – is equipped to land on the rock with one wave and immediately cement itself head downwards in its adult position before the next wave arrives to wash it away. This remarkably quick change enables the barnacle to use as its home the wave-battered headlands and vertical rock faces which few other animals can exploit.

This, then, is the sea-shore – a rich and varied habitat where we can find so many different creatures perfectly adapted to every inch of living-space and effectively using all the resources of this narrow but fascinating strip between the sea and the land.

Populations on the move

George S. Cansdale

Some animals live out their entire lives within a few miles of where they are born, but others travel vast distances each year across whole continents and oceans. Why do they migrate? How do they know where to go? How can they survive such long and exhausting journeys?

The term migration is not defined by distance – for some animals travel no more than a few hundred miles – but by the regular, cyclical nature of the journey. This cycle often takes place within the span of a single year, and its purpose is generally the search for food, followed by the return to the breeding-grounds. The true migrant is one who travels and returns, who has both a winter and a summer home.

What sorts of creatures migrate?

Birds are the greatest migrants – particularly when judged by the distances involved. The Arctic tern, for instance, is known to make an annual journey equivalent to one complete circumference of the equator (some 25,000 miles – over 40,000km).

The reindeer – the only member of the deer family to live in the Arctic region – moves south every autumn before the harsh winter sets in, returning again in spring when the days grow longer and warmer. Further south, on the African plains, the antelopes also migrate with the seasons, searching for the right kind of grasses.

Man too can be a migrant. In the Negev desert, for instance, whole families of Bedouin can be seen on the move, leading their live-stock to new water and pasture. In Iran and

Two contrasting immigrant peoples: the Lapps who follow the reindeer, and camel caravans in Iraq, moving in search of pasture.

Iraq there are tribes which migrate from the plains to the hills for the summer, and back again for the winter, all the time seeking fresh green grass for their sheep. In Lapland, the close relationship between the Lapps and the migrating reindeer provides us with a clear example of the way in which man can influence and utilize the cyclical migration of an animal species without destroying it.

Even insects migrate. Tropical butterflies and the dreaded locusts travel in swarms of many thousands or millions. But perhaps the strangest

journeys of all are those undertaken by certain fish.

The mystery of the eel

The eel is so long and thin and snake-like that many people do not realize that it is in fact a fish. There are many kinds of eel, most not more than 3 feet / 1 metre in length, although one of the sea species (the conger eel) grows to perhaps five times that size.

For many centuries, indeed until about forty

Development and migration of eel larvae

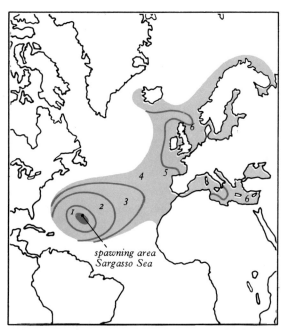

Leptocephalus larva of the European eel.

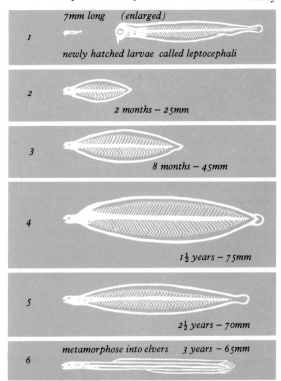

Later they grow into transparent elvers.

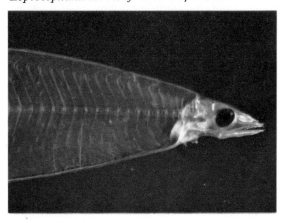

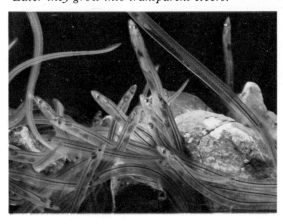

years ago, the European eel was something of a mystery to the experts. There were eels in every stream and pond, yet they never seemed to lay eggs and no baby eels were ever found. Then, from time to time, fully-grown eels were seen wriggling through wet grass far from their ponds.

Why had they left the water, and where were they going? Most of these cross-country eels were seen in spring, and in the same season fishermen noticed that many, most of them fully grown, were moving down the rivers towards the sea. Many were caught in basket traps set across the streams, but those that escaped and reached the sea simply disappeared.

The call of the sea

That was all we knew. Where they went and how long the journey took remained a mystery until scientists began to make a study of the small creatures that live in the ocean. It is not very easy to observe such tiny creatures, especially when they are deep down in the sea. Ordinary fishing-nets were far too coarse, so the scientists made very fine ones and towed these behind their boats at different depths.

Among the many creatures they caught were some tiny fish – an inch (250mm) or so long, flat and almost transparent. At first these were given a name of their own, but as the experts studied their specimens they noticed that the smallest were always caught far out at sea and the largest were found near to land.

The mystery is solved

As soon as it was realized that these tiny fish – growing larger as they approached land – were

Salmon migration area

Atlantic Ocean

nothing other than baby eels that would change their shape when they left the sea and moved into the fresh water, the mystery of the eel was nearly solved.

The place where the tiniest of the eel larvae were found – in the Sargasso Sea just north of the West Indies – must be the breeding-ground and therefore the end of the journey for the 'disappearing' eel. It is now believed indeed that the European eels, and also those from North America all make their way to this same small area of sea in the Atlantic Ocean.

Here they lay their millions of eggs, and then die. The eggs hatch, and the baby eels head back towards the rivers and ponds from which their parents came. The American eel takes only a year to reach land, but Europe is much farther away and the eels drifting that way in the Gulf Stream can take up to three and a half years over their journey.

Little by little we find out what happens,

The growth of a salmon

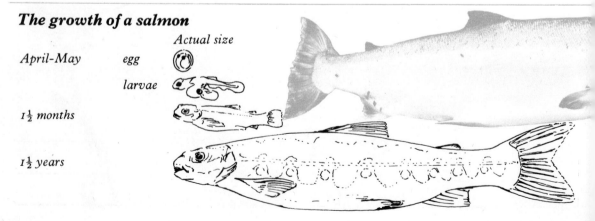

Actual size

April-May   egg

                   larvae

1½ months

1½ years

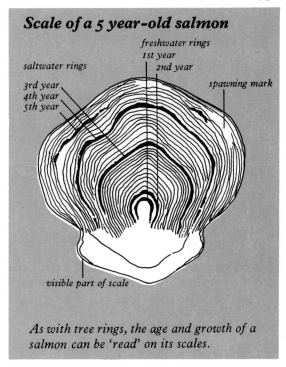

Scale of a 5 year-old salmon

saltwater rings

freshwater rings
1st year
2nd year

3rd year
4th year
5th year

spawning mark

visible part of scale

As with tree rings, the age and growth of a salmon can be 'read' on its scales.

A salmon leaping up river.

but we are often unable to answer the question, why? What makes these creatures set out on such vast journeys, only to have their paths retraced by the young they have spawned before dying? We can only wonder at the detail and complexity of the world of animals which God has made.

The journey in reverse

Another fish well worth studying is the salmon, whose size (up to 60lbs/27kg) and taste makes it so popular with fishermen and gourmets. Its life-cycle is the exact reverse of the eel's, for it is born in the rivers and grows to adult form out at sea.

While still at sea, it builds up a store of fat flesh which it will use up during the long journey to the fresh-water streams and rivers. Once there, it seeks out just the right kind of stony river bed, and lays up to 10,000 eggs, each the size of a pea.

First the female uses her body to cut a long shallow hole in the bed of small stones. As

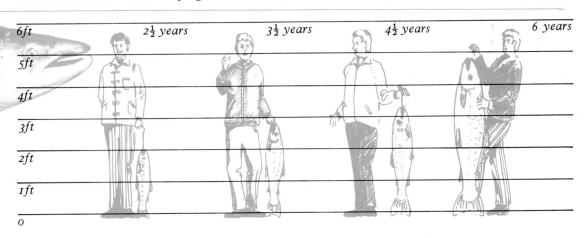

6ft   2½ years   3½ years   4½ years   6 years

5ft

4ft

3ft

2ft

1ft

0

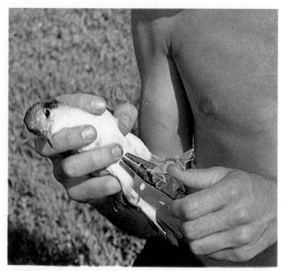

A light identification ring is put round the leg of a young arctic tern. Later the bird can be caught again and its movements accurately plotted.

The European stork. In ancient times the stork was used as a symbol of the traveller.

she lays her eggs into this hole, a male fish alongside fertilizes them. Then the fish carefully covers the eggs with small stones so as to let the water flow around without washing them away. By this time it is winter and the cold river water is full of the oxygen that the eggs need.

Once the eggs are laid, the work of the adult salmon is finished. Weak and exhausted by the journey and the egg-laying, they drop back towards the sea. Although most die before reaching it, a few manage to return to their feeding-grounds out at sea, where they grow strong and fat again before making a second journey to their river.

The unexplained urge

The baby salmon stays in the river for about two years, by which time it is as long as a man's hand. Then it begins to feel the urge to go out to sea. Just why or how it feels this need for salt water we do not know, but it sets off to the river mouth, where it joins up with young salmon from other rivers, all making their way up to a part of the North Atlantic near Greenland.

It is quite remarkable that they go to an area so rich in good food that within about two years they grow from almost nothing to perhaps 20lb/9kg – and there are not many kinds of fish that grow at that rate.

Unlike the eel when it goes to sea, the salmon

makes a return journey, and so tiny numbered labels can be fixed on the small fish before they go down river. Not many survive, but some come back and are caught – and we then know how long they have been away. These little labels also show that most salmon return to exactly the stream where they were hatched from eggs up to six years before. It seems that their sense of smell may help them to find the right river, but nothing other than an inherited pattern could take them on their first journey to their feeding-grounds.

The greatest migrants of all

Counting birds on the move is an almost impossible job, but experts have recently calculated that nearly 4,000 million birds fly down from Europe and western Asia to spend the northern winter in Africa, most of them staying north of the equator.

There are various routes over the Mediterranean but many birds – particularly those that visit West Africa – choose the short crossing over the Straits of Gibraltar. Others travel by way of the Nile Valley, and so have no sea crossing at all. This route passes over Israel and it was there that the prophet Jeremiah watched them some 2,500 years ago, writing perhaps the very first report about bird migration: 'Even the stork in the heavens knows her times; and the turtledove, swallow, and crane keep the time of their coming.'

Israel stands roughly where Europe, Asia and Africa meet. This is still at the cross-roads for these birds, and when their breeding season is

Location and migration of flamingos

- - - - - migration area

Flamingos live in enormous colonies around the shores of lakes. One colony in East Africa is known to number at least a million pairs.

Flamingos strain out their food by pumping the lake water through a 'sieve' formed by holding the thick tongue against ridges on the upper jaw.

over they make their way there from central and eastern Europe, as well as from western Asia, before flying on south. Central Africa, with its great lakes, is a major gathering-place. Flying insects are so plentiful that the new arrivals seem to make no impression on them, and there are enough fish in the warm waters to satisfy even the huge pelicans which have come from their breeding-grounds at the mouth of the River Danube, in the Black Sea.

Even in the age of the jet plane these are quite long journeys, yet some birds travel much farther still. The Arctic tern, a member of the gull family, feeds by diving into the water to catch small fish. It has a wide breeding range, although some nest within 500 miles/800km of the North Pole. As soon as the young ones are independent, the terns fly south. They cross Canada and the United States, then head across the Atlantic to the West African coast, where they rest and feed for a few days. Soon they set off again to the Antarctic, and here they spend several months on the edge of the sea ice before returning to their nesting-grounds. In the space of a single year, these birds travel a distance roughly equal to the circumference of the earth at the equator.

Birds share one problem with aeroplanes – they need fuel for the journey! Terns have a chance of fishing from time to time, but many small birds have to cross the seas without stopping. For instance, a little humming-bird flies across the Gulf of Mexico in spring and back again in the autumn – about 500 miles/800km each way – and to prepare for this it stores up special foods in its muscles. By the end of the flight it is down to half its original weight.

Many of the larger birds save fuel by gliding much of the way and this means travel overland, for – like the glider pilot – they depend on the thermal currents to give them a free lift to several thousand feet ready for a further long glide.

How do they find their way?

It was only when birds were given little numbered rings or bands that we began to find out some firm facts about migration. Over the years enough birds are recovered to tell us a lot about them – where they go and by what routes; whether they return to their nesting-places; how long the various kinds of birds live, and so on.

But one thing ringing cannot tell us is how they find their way. Scientists have been studying this for a long time and while they have not yet found the whole answer they now know that birds use several methods. Those that travel fairly small distances mostly use their eyes. This is true, for instance, of pigeons. They are taken on longer and longer training flights so that they can learn their surroundings and so find their way back home.

But this cannot possibly be true of the long-distance travellers, especially those that fly across hundreds of miles of sea, out of sight of land and often at night. Nor is it true of those birds whose young, when only a few months old, fly south several weeks after their parents have left. This is what happens with cuckoos, yet these young birds winter in the same parts of Africa as their parents and return, the next spring, to more or less the place where they were hatched.

This can only mean that birds have a built-in memory of where to go and that they have the means to navigate. Scientists have used all sorts of modern apparatus in their research, including radar and planetaria. They have concluded that birds have a memory of star patterns and sun position, and also a very accurate sense of time.

Many details are not yet clear, and it seems that they vary from one kind of bird to another, but the truth is this – that these birds do by instinct what man needs complicated instruments and very accurate clocks to do for him. Long before Jeremiah made those observations about birds migrating over the Holy Land, and long before man had worked out the first simple method of finding his way across the ocean, these birds had been coming and going on their long journeys.

We know that the young eel may take up to three and a half years to travel from the Atlantic to Europe; that salmon know how to find just the right sort of fresh-water breeding-grounds and where to head for in search of food; that birds can find their way over vast distances. But we cannot often say *why*. All we can say is that this is just part of the amazing variety in the world of animals that God has made, each wonderfully fitted for its particular style of life, however strange that life-style may seem to us humans – and that the Creator who made these animals also gave them just the right senses and instincts to let them undertake such difficult and mysterious journeys.

Eyes and ears, colours and sounds

Timothy J. Stevenson

If red and green make yellow, why don't a squeak and a groan make a hoot?

Perhaps that question should be asked again more carefully! Colours can easily be mixed to make other colours, but it is not often that two sounds mix together to make a quite different one. Why do sounds have this power to remain themselves even among other sounds?

Maybe you do not even believe that red and green make yellow, so that is a good place to start. If you had two torches, one with a red bulb and one with a green bulb, you could do the experiment shown in the picture. Where both red and green light falls on the white card you see yellow. The important thing is that it is *light* that is being mixed. In one sense, light is the only thing that can be coloured. Nothing is

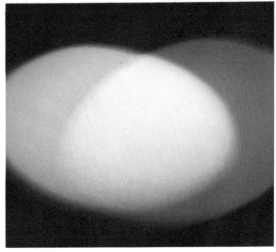

Mixing red and green light produces yellow on the white card. The two coloured lights must be of similiar intensity or the yellow will look brownish or washed out.

coloured in the dark! Under pure yellow light, the sort that comes from some street lamps, everything seems yellow.

Coloured light

Unless they are glowing hot, things only seem coloured because they reflect some colours of light and not others. Things seem fully coloured in white light because white is a mixture of all the colours. This can be proved by using a triangle of glass called a prism to split up a narrow beam of white light. You can see how the prism bends the light that goes through it. The red part of white light is bent by a certain amount, the orange part by a bit more, the yellow part by even more, and so on through all the colours of the rainbow. This sorting out of all the different colours in light is called a spectrum.

One way in which we can all see a spectrum of white light is by looking at a rainbow. Here drops of water split the light up. The light bounces around inside the drops, and different colours come out in different directions. For the drops that are in one part of the rainbow, the red light comes out in the right direction to reach your eyes. That part of the sky looks red. Drops in other parts of the sky send other colours to your eyes, and in this way you see a spectrum, or rainbow.

This also explains why you can never walk through a rainbow. The drops only seem coloured because they are in the right place to send coloured light to your eyes. If you move, a different place becomes the right place. The right place moves with you; that is to say the rainbow moves with you. The easiest way of trying this for yourself is to find a baby rainbow in a spray of water from a hose on a sunny day. You will see the rainbow in the spray if the sun is behind you.

Mixing colours

Do red and green really make yellow? Red and green paints mix to give a muddy brown, don't they? Mixing paint is not the same thing as mixing light. Red paint reflects red light and absorbs (swallows up) the rest. Green paint absorbs everything except green light. Mixed together they absorb nearly everything. Just a tiny bit of yellow light escapes to give that muddy brown.

Even so, do red and green really make yellow? Nothing can split up pure yellow light into any other colours. If you mix pure red and green light, what you see is just like yellow, but if you pass it through a prism you get back red and green – no yellow at all.

The answer to this puzzle is in the way our eyes see colour. They do not tell us everything about the light we see. The cells at the back of our eyes make just three measurements of any colour – how much red, how much green, how much blue. Yellow comes between red and green in the spectrum, and it causes both the red-measuring cells and the green-measuring cells to send messages to our brains. Because a mixture of red and green light causes exactly the same messages, we cannot tell the difference between this mixture and pure yellow.

Light through a prism

Because the different colours of light bend different amounts in a prism, white light can be split up into its constituent colours. Purple bends the most, and red the least.

A prism does not break up pure yellow light.

It does separate a yellow mixture (i.e. red + green) back to the original two colours.

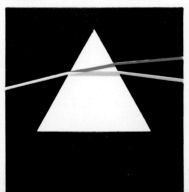

Oscilloscope graphs

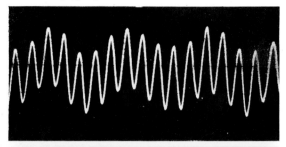

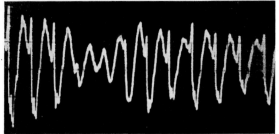

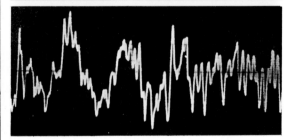

The rainbow of sound

Just as there is a spectrum of light from red to violet, there is a spectrum of sound from the deepest growl to the highest squeak.

We hear sound when the air vibrates – that is, moves rapidly backwards and forwards. The lowest sounds we hear are when the air goes backwards and forwards about thirty times a second. The highest sounds are between 15,000 and 20,000 vibrations a second. Big, heavy and floppy things vibrate slowly and make deep sounds.

Look at the wiggles in the picture. These were made with a microphone connected to an electronic instrument called an oscilloscope. They show the way the air moves to and fro when sound passes through it. The sound shown in the top picture is a whistle, the middle one is someone speaking and the bottom one is paper tearing. Would you have guessed what they were? If you had heard the sounds you would have known at once.

The oscilloscope pictures describe how the air moves in a jerky sort of a way when sound goes through it. That is what happens, that is *all* that happens, but these pictures are not the only or the best description of sound. They mean nothing when you look at them. If a composer wrote his music down like that, who could play it? For us it is much more natural to think of sounds, especially musical ones, as mixtures of higher and lower notes, rather than as wavy lines.

Having it both ways!

To understand how these two ways of thinking about sound fit together we must look at some more wiggles. First a bit more explanation of what they mean may be useful.

In the picture you can see a nice, rather old-fashioned experiment. The tuning fork marked D is twanged so that it vibrates, giving out sound. The cylinder is covered with lampblack (soot from an oil lamp or candle) which the

A spectrometer

The prism in an instrument called a spectrometer can be used to measure the exact wavelength of light given off by objects or gases. In this way light from distant stars can now be analysed to show what materials they are composed of.

For example pure hydrogen emits visible light of only five different wavelengths. These appear as narrow lines or bands on the spectroscope. These can be used to detect the presence of a gas as surely as a finger print identifies a criminal.

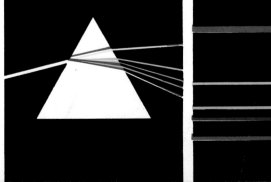

needle can scrape off. In this way the machine can make a wavy line which is a picture of the sound of the tuning fork. (G in the picture is a rod which is also twanged to give a record of another sound for comparison.)

The first gramophone records were made on machines rather like this, with some arrangement so that the sound to be recorded made the needle vibrate. Of course the cylinder had to be covered in something better than soot, or any attempt to play it back would have ruined it!

Now look at the next picture. The top line represents what is, in a way, the simplest sound possible. This is called a sine wave or, in musical language, a pure tone. The sounds of a flute or a tuning fork are rather like it. The next four lines are more sine waves, just the same only faster. The bottom line is what you get if you mix all the others together. It is a quite uneven shape. It is a very important and useful fact that you can make a line any shape you like by adding enough sine waves together. To put it another way, you can make any sound you like by mixing enough pure tones. It takes more sine waves to make up a jagged line than to make a smooth one. A jagged line would come from a harsh sound.

There are, then, two quite different ways of describing a sound. The first is to say how the air actually moves. The second is to give the recipe for making the sound out of pure tones. Each description is complete and accurate, but they have different uses.

It is important to be able to describe things from different points of view like this. Some scientists may say 'Only my description is right' – but other descriptions may be just as true as well. For instance, people can be described as complicated mechanisms – but not *just* as mechanisms. This scientific description is true. But it is just as true to describe a person in other terms – as being a friend, or as loving other people, for example.

Sounds in tune

We have seen how our ears treat a sound as a mixture of pure tones. This helps us to understand some of the interesting things about music. Sometimes two instruments playing different notes can blend together so that it seems as if there is only one sound. Why does this happen, when it is not usual for sounds to mix, as we

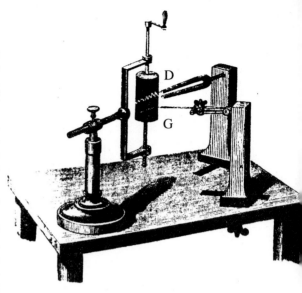

Duhamel's graphic method, great-grandfather of the record player!

Sine waves

said at the beginning? Why do notes that are in tune sound right, and notes out of tune sound wrong?

The answer to these puzzles is that, as we have seen, each musical sound is made up of a whole series of pure tones. These tones are usually called the harmonics of the sound. If the harmonics, the tones that make up one sound are almost the same as the harmonics of another, then you would expect the sound to be similar. Musical sounds that are in tune with each other and blend together do in fact have some harmonics in common.

The deepest harmonic of simple musical sound is called the fundamental. Of course it will be a sine wave with a certain number of vibrations every second. Another harmonic will have twice as many vibrations, another three times as many, and so on. We call the number of vibrations in a second the frequency.

Now think what happens if there is a second note whose fundamental has a frequency twice as big as the frequency of the fundamental of the first note. The fundamental of the second note is the same as one of the harmonics of the first note. In fact all the harmonics of the first note may also be found in the second one. Not surprisingly, these notes sound good together. They are an octave apart, in musical language. On the other hand, two sounds that are out of tune will have quite different harmonics. For this reason they will not sound comfortable together, and a listener who has practised enough can easily sort them out.

Our ears are very good at sorting out sounds, our eyes are not nearly as good at sorting out colours. Part of the reason for this is that our ears do not tell us very exactly where a sound is coming from. This means that they can concentrate on measuring very carefully what it is. They have a rather wonderful little mechanism for doing this. Our eyes on the other hand can measure the colour and the position of hundreds of things at once, so it is not surprising that the colour measurements have to be fairly simple. Eyes and ears together combine to give us a remarkably clear and complete picture of the world we live in.

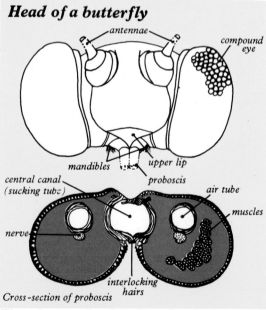

Head of a butterfly

antennae

compound eye

mandibles   upper lip

central canal (sucking tube)

proboscis

air tube

nerve

muscles

interlocking hairs

Cross-section of proboscis

These close-ups show how the proboscis of a butterfly is composed of two halves which join to form a long narrow sucking tube.

The spider and the fly

Barbara Drake

A delicate spider's web sparkling with dew is a beautiful sight in the early morning. But although it gives us such pleasure, that sticky web is a terrible trap for any insect that blunders into it.

While the insect struggles to free itself, the waiting spider injects a paralyzing venom. Then he parcels up his helpless victim in a cocoon of threads, so that he can suck the precious body fluids at his leisure. All that is left of the insect in the end is a dry, lifeless husk.

A juicy morsel!

Bees, butterflies, mosquitoes and many other small creatures also feed on plant or animal juices, extracting them with mouth-parts ingeniously adapted to the purpose. Plant juices are very nourishing and easy to digest. They are rich in sugars and contain some amino-acids. Animal juices are solutions of proteins. They contain less carbohydrate than a plant's juices, but provide a good food supply.

The simplest way for an animal to feed on juices is to crush its prey and suck up the juices which exude from it. This is how many spiders, scorpions and other arachnids feed. A scorpion will hold its prey between large 'pincers' or pedipalps and chew it, sucking up the juices through the pharynx. But this is by no means the only way that insects obtain their food.

Specially equipped

The insect family is one of the biggest and most diverse in the animal kingdom. Within it there is a wide variety of design, down to the smallest detail. Each is beautifully suited to its own way of living. The 'limbs' attached to the

The long proboscis of a butterfly, specially designed to reach deep down into a flower and draw up nectar.
When not in use, the proboscis coils up again under the butterfly's head.

head of an insect are specially adapted as mouth-parts to suit various ways of feeding – biting, piercing, sucking – and various sorts of food. A chewing insect, for example, has very hard jaws with teeth for biting.

Nectar and the bees

The mouth-parts of other insects are specially adapted for sucking up juices. These insects are attracted by the bright colours and enticing scents of flowering plants but most of all by the sweet juice, the nectar, which they can gather from them. The bee is an obvious example.

Nectar is an important food for the bee community. Worker bees have mouth-parts specially suited to their work of collecting nectar and moulding wax, whereas the mouth-parts of the queen bee and the drones, who do not collect nectar are shorter. Honey bees have 'tongues'. Some are short-tongued, some long-tongued, suiting them to different flowers.

When the bee visits a flower it alights on the top and forages about, dipping its tongue down to the base of the petals until it finds the nectar. It extends its tongue by the pressure of blood forced from the head into the cavity. Under a microscope, we can see that the bee's tongue is not flat. It has its edges rolled over until they nearly meet in the middle to form a tube. The bore of this tube is small enough for liquid to rise up it by capillary action, and the movement of the liquid is aided by a shortening of the tongue which forces liquid higher up. All this is further aided by the sucking action of the pharynx, which has special muscles to increase its volume.

Butterflies and moths

Butterflies and moths are almost as efficient as the bees at collecting nectar. Their 'tongues' are much longer and are formed of two half tubes which make a complete tube when locked together.

A meal with the insects

1. The shiny beetle *Cryptocephalus aureolus* munches a buttercup petal.

2. An Elephant Hawk moth caterpillar feeding on a leaf.

3. A shield bug tackles a caterpillar.

4. The larva of a Great Diving beetle has caught a tadpole in its sickle-shaped jaws.

5. A mantis makes a meal out of an unwary beetle.

6. The Orb Weaver spider feeding on a Paper wasp.

An ant with its 'flock' of honeydew-producing aphids.

When not in use this sucking proboscis is coiled up beneath the head, where it can most often be seen. The hairs on the forefeet sense the sugars and the signal from these sense cells causes a rise in blood pressure which uncoils the proboscis. As the two halves are held together by an arrangement of overlapping pieces and interlocking hairs the tube is watertight, and the liquid can be sucked up by the action of the pharangeal pump. The insect probes with the end of the extended proboscis, which suggests that it can use the tip for sensing the right place from which to collect food.

Green-fly on the roses

Of course nectar is not the only source of liquid food; plant cells are full of nutrient liquids, although the cellulose cell walls are not digestible and are very tough. However there are many insects which can bore or cut a way through the cell wall to reach the juices inside. Leaf-hoppers, frog-hoppers, scale insects, cochineal insects and cicadas all feed in this way. So do the much more common aphids.

Aphids are well known to the gardener, and are not a welcome friend! They are white or green, and can be seen massed on the new green shoots of plants. These insects have needle-like mouth-parts with which they can penetrate the outer layers of a leaf, root or stem, and secrete salivery juices into the plant which break down the cell walls. The liquid food can then be sucked up. These mouth-parts are sometimes so long that they are coiled in a sac beneath the head and can be inserted a long way into a plant.

Ants can often be seen running over and around aphids. This is because the aphids extract more plant juices than they need. They excrete the surplus sugar as 'honeydew' – a favourite food of the ants.

Blood-suckers and spreaders of disease

The activities of these insects, annoying and destructive as they are, do not affect us as much as the habits of some blood-sucking insects. At the mention of bed-bugs or fleas, or even mosquitoes, we humans begin to look uncomfortable and even begin to scratch! The mouth-parts

Lesser houseflies on the bacon.

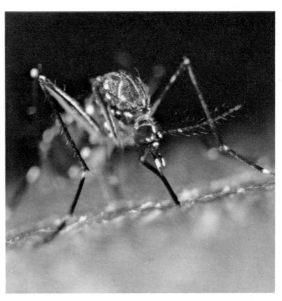

A mosquito feeding. You can see the blood it has sucked up in its red stomach.

of these insects have to be very sharp indeed to pierce the tough skin of humans and animals.

The mosquito's razor-sharp jaws pierce the flesh and make the wound. It then injects saliva containing anti-coagulants into the wound, allowing the blood to flow freely. The insect gorges itself until its whole body is distended with blood. If the mosquito is carrying the malaria parasite, the parasite will pass with the saliva into the bloodstream of the bitten animal or human and infect the liver and the red blood cells.

The tsetse fly also feeds on blood, and is a carrier of sleeping sickness – a dreaded disease in West and Central Africa.

Closer to home, another more familiar disease-spreading insect is the common housefly. This is a lazy insect. It relies on the food we leave about. The housefly lives on fluid foods. Its mouth-parts are in the form of a pad with food channels passing from the outer edge to the middle. When this pad is put down into the liquid, it can be sucked up through the channels and into the mouth. This fly can also deal with solid food, such as sugar, which will dissolve easily. It exudes a drop of fluid from its proboscis or 'tongue' on the sugar. This dissolves, and the sugary fluid is sucked up.

A fly may have been feeding on fluids from animal waste or dung before it settles on exposed human food. The drop of fluid from the fly's gut or alimentary canal and the sticky pads on the fly's feet often carry disease-causing germs. Such germs may give rise to dysentery, diarrhoea or other digestive troubles. This is why food should be kept covered and the housefly controlled.

Scientists who have looked at the 'engineering' of insect mouth-parts have been amazed at their perfection and intricacy. The parts dovetail or slide smoothly over one another with a mechanism so superb that the finest modern engineering cannot surpass it.

The instinct for survival

George S. Cansdale

In an earlier chapter, we saw how some birds, fish and four-footed animals travel great distances in order to find just the right conditions for the different seasons of the year. But what happens to those animals which cannot swim or fly, or do not have the strength to move far across land? How do they survive when life becomes difficult?

Those of us who live in warm, temperate climates often forget that elsewhere in the world animal and plant life has a fight for survival against extremes of heat and cold.

Extremes in the desert

The desert is a thoroughly uncomfortable place to live in. For much of the year it is extremely hot by day and cold by night. But although deserts may look dead, most of them support an amazing amount of animal as well as plant life. Snakes, lizards, rodents and different kinds of insects are only a few of the creatures which have their own survival techniques, enabling them to live in desert conditions.

In order to survive, these creatures must adapt even their times of activity – the vital search for food – to the extremes of killing heat by day and cold at night. Except perhaps for part of the cooler season, the ground surface during the day becomes much too hot for safety, so the small animals have to spend the daytime underground or in cracks in the rocks.

Animals and birds are able to adapt to the most adverse living-conditions.
A dove has built her nest in a cactus plant.
A snake in the Kalahari Desert.
A delicate flower that blooms immediately after rain and dies one day later.

The Sahara Desert. At an oasis, where there is water, plants can spring up and survive the heat.

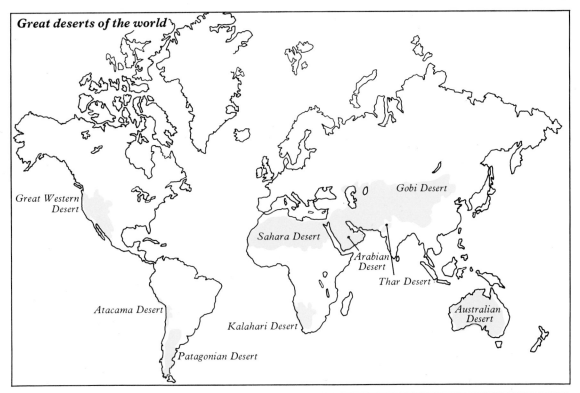

Great deserts of the world

Great Western Desert
Atacama Desert
Patagonian Desert
Sahara Desert
Kalahari Desert
Gobi Desert
Arabian Desert
Thar Desert
Australian Desert

Water storage in the desert

The Saguaro cactus stores water in its pulpy stem. In a drought its pleated trunk shrinks slowly as the water is used up.

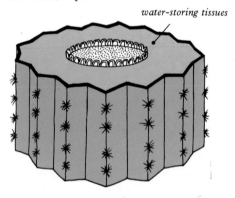

water-storing tissues

After rain the storage tissues fill up and the trunk is plump again.

Sometimes the nights are bitterly cold – too cold for the small animals to be active, so they search for food in the evening, when the ground is cooling down, and in the morning, when it is warming up.

But that is not all. There may be a season when the weather is extra hot and then the temperature hardly drops, even at night.

In North Africa the temperature may be as much as 38°C (100°F) at midnight! This is more than most of the desert mice, the snakes and the lizards can take, so they go into a special kind of sleep, in the safety of their underground holes, where the air is cooler and not so dry. It is almost as if they are just 'ticking over', like an idling engine, using up very little energy. They can stay like this for weeks at a time, if need be, until the worst of the heat is over.

A lesson from the ant

It is surprising how often the animal world has something to teach us about life. Look at the way the insects survive in the desert. The cold part of the winter is no problem to them, for they simply become inactive, staying in the safety of their underground nests. This is a similar state to winter sleep, or hibernation.

But these insects also have to survive a season when the weather is so hot and dry that many plants stop growing and life for small creatures becomes very difficult indeed.

Long ago, when he wanted to teach his people a lesson about being prepared and thinking ahead, Solomon, king of Israel, told them to go and watch the ant.

In the spring and early summer the ants gather seeds of various kinds, especially grass seeds, and carry them back to the nest. There, to save storage space, they take off all the husks and leave them to be blown away by the wind. Then, when the hot weather comes, the ants can stay underground, where it is cooler and damper, and live on their stores.

Waiting for the signal

Some of these desert climates follow no regular pattern. They can be very unpredictable, and this presents the animals with different problems.

A year or more may pass without any rain and then everything seems dead. But if you dug deep

Leaf-Cutter ants busily carrying away small pieces of leaf to make compost underground. On this they grow the 'mushrooms' on which they feed.

in the ground you would find the plant roots far from dead, just waiting for water before springing into active life again. You might also find lots of insect eggs, especially locusts' and grasshoppers'.

Unlike most eggs, these do not hatch automatically after a certain number of days or months. They can stay safely buried for month after month – some for as long as seven years – just waiting for a signal. That signal is rain. When rain falls the plants will come alive again and within a few days or weeks the grasshoppers will emerge – in time to enjoy a meal of green leaves. Had they hatched in the ordinary way, there would have been nothing for them to eat and all would have died.

Fish with lungs?

One of the things that happens in hot countries is that from time to time the streams and lakes dry up. Of course this presents serious problems to the animals living there. Some fish manage to swim to deeper places where they will be safe. Other species of fish, and in particular the smaller creatures, survive by leaving eggs which can wait dried up for months and months, and then hatch at once when the rains come.

But there is one large fish in Central Africa,

The desert locust, whose eggs hatch only after rain.

and others very like it in America and Australia, with its own special way of surviving, even when the river or lake has dried up completely.

It is called a lung fish. This sounds all wrong, because we know that fish do not have lungs. Deep inside the body of every fish is a tiny bag filled with air. This is called the swim bladder, because it is used for keeping the fish at the right depth in the water. But in the lung fish this has become a sort of lung by which it can make use of air. Of course, like all fishes, it still has gills. These gills are situated just behind the head, and fish use them to take oxygen out of the water. But even in ordinary times the lung fish comes to the surface of the water to take a mouthful of air for the swim bladder.

When the river or lake starts to dry up, the lung fish burrows down into the mud and bends itself into the shape of a letter 'U'. It produces an extra supply of that slimy substance that normally covers its skin, and this dries to form a sort of eggshell or case around it. A little tube leads

A hedgehog is a warm-blooded animal but food is scarce in winter, so he goes to sleep curled up into a tight ball.

from this shell to the surface of the mud, just big enough for air to pass through. And there the lung fish may wait for several months, using up hardly any of its food reserves, until the rain comes, and it can take to the water again.

Hazards of winter

Of course not all climates present their animals and insects with such extreme conditions. Yet even in more moderate – 'temperate' – climates, animals have their problems. The main one is how to survive the winter.

In winter time insects, and all other creatures without a backbone (invertebrates) die, or find a hiding-place until warm weather returns, or else they leave eggs which will hatch in the spring.

In Britain, for example, you never see snakes or lizards, frogs or tortoises moving about during the winter. These animals all hide or bury themselves in some place where they can sleep the cold months away.

This deep winter sleep is called hibernation. The animal's body is cold and seems lifeless, but when the warm weather comes it gradually wakes up again. Animals which hibernate are said to be 'cold-blooded', but this only means that they cannot regulate their temperature. They are therefore as cold or warm as their surroundings.

In contrast, the birds and furred animals are called 'warm-blooded' because they have a fairly even body temperature, however warm or cold it may be outside. This is because these creatures, like ourselves, have a built-in control – a thermostat.

Furry animals can therefore keep warm during the winter. But to do so they need plenty of food, and this can be a problem. Some of them find food so scarce that although they could keep warm, they go to sleep instead.

This is true, for instance, of the bat. Bats hunt and catch insects in the air, but in the cold weather they can find no insects to feed on, so they hide away in caves, old buildings or hollow trees – just the sort of places where they normally live in the daytime, hanging upside down.

In their deep winter sleep the bats' bodies are really cold, almost as if they had switched off their thermostats. Breathing almost stops and the heart beats so slowly that you cannot even feel it. The bat's reserves of food, stored away as fat in various parts of the body, last it through the winter. When spring arrives, the bat comes to life again, returns to normal temperature, and flies out to find a meal of insects.

Instinct or choice?

One of the things that distinguishes the human race from other animals is man's ability to plan and think ahead. Yet when we see how these animals prepare themselves for the onset of winter or of great heat, it seems almost as if they have more sense than we do!

Journey into cold

Timothy J. Stevenson

What happens when water freezes? Why does a pond start to freeze at the surface and not at the bottom? What is 'dry' ice? Can scientists cool a liquid to absolute zero?

These are the sort of questions which arise when we begin to think about subjecting liquids and other substances to intense cold. It is surprising how often the commonest everyday happenings turn out to be the strangest and most interesting of all the wonders of the created world. Take the way water changes into ice, for example.

Turning water into ice

There is nothing particularly unusual about a liquid changing into a solid; hundreds of substances can be altered in this way. What is strange about water is that as it freezes it expands or grows bigger. Almost everything else shrinks a little when it turns from liquid to solid. Water is different because the molecules or minute particles that it is made of are a rather awkward shape, and when they fit together to make ice they take up a lot of room. (See diagrams on pages 78 and 79.)

This may not seem particularly important – yet if water shrank as it froze, instead of expanding, the world would be a quite different place. For one thing, there would be no ice on top of ponds in winter.

Think what happens to a bowl of cooking fat as it cools down. The fat starts to go solid from the bottom upwards. If water did not expand as it froze, that is what would happen to a pond.

Frozen fish and sinking icebergs!

As it is, the layer of ice on top of a pond acts as a sort of blanket, slowing down further freezing. Without this protective covering a pond would freeze much more quickly, and that would be the end of quite a lot of fish.

If water shrank when it froze, icebergs, instead of floating, would sink to the bottom of the ocean. If all the ice at the North Pole sank, then the sea currents, the height of the sea, the weather and who knows what else would be different. Such changes at the North Pole would make any little bother with frozen fish seem insignificant by comparison.

Walking on ice

Another thing would be different if water did not expand as it froze: ice would not be slippery. There is a scientific principle (known as Le Chatelier's Principle) which says, in effect, that a thing goes the way you push it – although it is usually put in more careful and ponderous language ('if a system in equilibrium is subject to a stress, the system tends to react in such a way as to oppose the effect of the stress').

It is quite easy and obvious really, as the example of slippery ice shows. When it freezes, water expands. If you squash it enough, it will melt again. This means that when you tread on ice, a thin layer of water forms where your shoe squashes it. This water acts as a lubricant, just like oil. But unlike oil, it is formed just where it is most needed, at the point where the pressure is greatest.

If freezing water did not expand, none of this would happen and – unless your shoes were hot enough to melt it – ice would be no more slippery than stone. Ice can get so cold that no amount of squashing can melt it, and then you can neither slip nor skate on it.

Dry ice

Another unusual cold substance is 'dry ice', which is formed when the gas carbon dioxide is cooled below minus 78°C. Dry ice gets its name from the fact that when it is heated it does not melt, but turns straight to gas.

If you put a piece of dry ice on a table, the heat from the table makes it turn into gas. To use

The film of water on the cold glass of a window freezes into patterns which look like leaves or feathers.

the language of science, it 'sublimes'. As it sublimes, the gas being formed underneath it lifts it slightly off the table and it slithers about rather like a tiny hovercraft.

Colder and yet colder

At minus 183°C, oxygen turns to liquid, and at minus 196° the same thing happens to nitrogen. At temperatures like these rubber becomes hard and brittle, so that you can break it with a hammer; lead, usually a fairly soft metal, becomes hard and springy.

At colder temperatures still, everything freezes, goes solid, stops. Heat is nothing more than a vibration of molecules, and when you remove it you slow down almost everything. This, of course, is why we have refrigerators – in order to slow down the process of food going bad.

At minus 196° (the temperature of liquid nitrogen) things keep almost for ever. This is true even for simple living things, although there are some big problems in cooling them down in a way which does not kill them.

The last gas to turn liquid is helium, at a temperature of minus 269°. At just two degrees below this, liquid helium becomes very creepy stuff indeed – quite literally. It is able to crawl up over the rim of any little cup you put it in, and drips down from the bottom of the cup. It can also creep through the tiniest crack with ease – in fact the tinier the crack the better. Of course all these experiments have to be carried out in very special apparatus in order to keep everything so cold.

Electricity without waste

Other strange things happen at these low temperatures. Normally something – a battery or a generator – is needed to make electricity flow along a wire. When some metals are made very cold, then suddenly this is no longer true. An electric current can go on flowing for ever. But this current cannot be used to run a bulb or heater, for that would stop it at once.

This strange behaviour, which is known as superconductivity, is very useful in making

A demonstration of water density

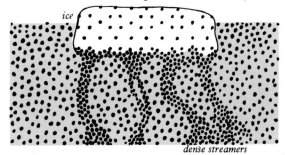

ice

dense streamers

Because ice is less dense than water, an ice-cube can be floated in a tank of warmer water. As it melts it forms extremely cold water in which the molecules are very close together. As this is heavier than the surrounding water it can be seen streaming downwards.

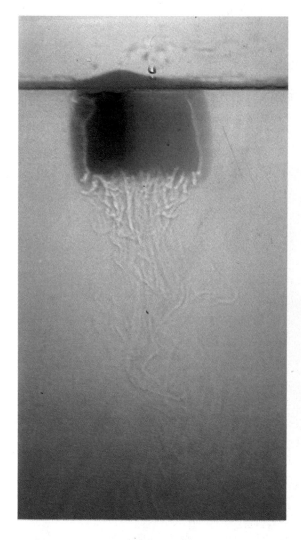

Each of the liquids in these three vacuum insulated Dewar flasks (the chemist's equivalent of the Thermos flask) is boiling at room temperature. From bottom to top they contain, respectively, liquid argon, oxygen and nitrogen. The low boiling-point of these liquids causes them to evaporate into their natural gaseous state when exposed to the normal heat of the lab. Water vapour in the air is frozen into icy cloud formations.

powerful magnets for scientific experiments. Before very long such magnets may be used in some of the generators that produce our electricity. Superconducting cables may be used to carry electricity around the country without wasting any heat in the way that the present cables do.

The absolute end

Our journey into cold ends at minus 273°C – the temperature we call absolute zero.

Heat in a substance is the vibration of its molecules. To cool it is to slow the molecules down. Absolute zero is the temperature at which they can be slowed down no further.

There is no limit to how hot a substance can be made. But you cannot be more stopped than stopped! You cannot make something colder than absolute zero.

In fact, although it is possible to cool something almost to absolute zero, you can never quite get there. Each tiny bit of heat is harder to remove than the last, even with the most powerful and intricate machines. And although you may be able to remove most of the heat in a substance, you can never remove it all.

At absolute zero life could not exist in any form. But at all temperatures above that there are, as we have seen, some fascinating experiments to be carried out in this complex and wonderful world.

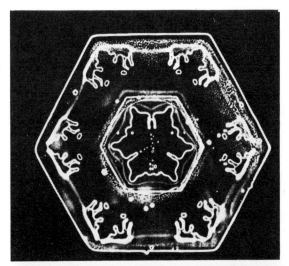

Snow can look beautiful, sparkling in the sun.

Each snowflake is composed of thousands of water crystals, each with its own pattern.

Icicles are formed when water freezes as it drips down from a roof or a branch. Each drop of water runs down the icicle but becomes so cold that it freezes at the tip instead of dropping off. In this way icicles can grow very long indeed.

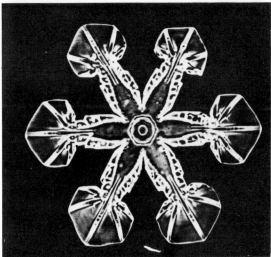

The balance of nature

F. Nigel Hepper

Does it matter if animal species die out? Can we not simply replace extinct species with others that still survive? Why not take whatever we need from nature? Surely there is always plenty more?

The chapters of this book have looked at many different aspects of the world around us. We have seen something of the variety of animal and plant life, and looked into the very origins of life and the tiniest cells that make up the basic substances.

Upsetting the scales

We have also seen how one part of nature depends on so many others. The natural world is like a carefully balanced pair of scales. Put too much weight on either side and the balance is upset. Unfortunately man tends to act in a heavy-handed, often unthinking way. By cutting and killing, burning and polluting, he is constantly upsetting the balance of nature.

Plants and animals living together in their natural surroundings depend on each other for food and shelter. But it is all too easy for man rapidly to change, or even destroy, this environment, giving the animals and plants no time to escape or adapt themselves to the new conditions.

Until quite recently people did not bother much about such problems. More and more people were coming to live in towns – what did the balance of the natural world matter? The increasing importance of Nature Reserves and National Parks shows that we are at last coming to our senses and beginning to appreciate the things we have so nearly destroyed. But even so these are only a small part of the whole surface of the earth. The rest is increasingly becoming changed and polluted.

The population explosion

There are now many more people in the world than there used to be, and each person needs

Our thoughtless misuse of the world around us has led to some horrible cases of pollution and destruction. Before clean air legislation, factory chimneys belched gas and fumes into the air over our cities.

to be fed and housed. Yet he also needs beauty around him and quiet places for leisure, so it is only right that we should make the best use of the land. Unfortunately this does not always

Oil from damaged tankers has made beaches unusable and killed much sea and shore life.

Cars and other manufactured goods are often *made in such a way that they are useless after a few years. Then comes the problem of how to dispose of them.*

A chemical plant empties its waste into the waterways.

Crop spraying can drastically upset the balance of nature if the instructions are not carefully followed.

happen, and a great deal of our natural resources are wasted and damaged. For example, whole forests have been cut down for timber, leaving the rain to wash away the soil unchecked. The result has been dry, barren hillsides and flooded valleys.

New crops and medicines

Of course nobody wants to starve the human population for the sake of a rare plant or animal. But at the same time, who knows which of today's wild plants could become a new crop plant in the future? When you think

millions of people

2000 AD — 6,000

— 5,000

The world population explosion

The graph shows the sharp rise in the human population over the past two hundred years.
In the last century the population doubled and it is believed that by 2000 it will have doubled again.

—— 4,000

1963 —— 3,000

1950
———— 2,000

1900

1850
1800 ——————————————————— 1,000
1750   750
1700   500
1650   250
AD 1   0

of it, our present-day crops, such as potatoes, cabbages and wheat, have been developed from wild ones. People have been growing them for hundreds of years, saving some of the seeds to be sown the following year. Sometimes the farmer has noticed an especially fruitful plant or one that grew better than the others, so little by little he has improved the crop.

Nowadays scientific plant breeding is rapidly developing wonderfully productive varieties – until a disease sweeps through the crop! Then the scientists need to breed newer varieties to resist the disease, and this can usually only be done by using some of the plant's wild relatives to reinvigorate the crop. So we see how important it is to have the wild plants available for this kind of work.

Did you know that not all medicines are produced from chemicals? Many are extracted

Since the trees take so long to grow, a fire in a deciduous forest can do literally hundreds of years of damage.

Soil erosion is often caused by the wholesale destruction of trees. Once the trees have gone the soil can easily be washed away by heavy rain, leaving a barren area where no new plants can grow. This picture was taken in Kenya.

Jungle land after fire. The land is scorched and bare, the Drypetes trees dead.

from plants, and scientists are working hard trying to find others. In fact, in their search for a cure for cancer, they are looking for drugs from wild tropical plants, and soon, if they are successful, important new crops could be developed from some of these. Unfortunately, some of these plants are vanishing even before they can be tested. Frequent fires prevent the growth of trees and heavy grazing by cattle changes the vegetation. Allowing soil to wash or blow away means that the plants are destroyed.

What can be done?

It is not easy to insist that fires should be less frequent or that cattle should be reduced in number when the people's way of life depends on them. Yet in East Africa interesting experiments have shown that the natural herds of wild animals produce more meat than herds of cows!

This is because the wild animals are of different kinds and sizes. Some need grass and small plants, others feed on bushes, and some, such as the tall giraffe, live off acacia trees. When the herds grow too large, their meat can be used for food. This means that the animals are not replaced by cows and that the vegetation, with its various kinds of plants, must be preserved as their food supply.

In the moister parts of the tropics the forests are rich with many different kinds of plants and animals. But the balance is more easily upset there than in the conifer forests of northern lands. The demand for timber is now so great that these temperate forests cannot supply all we need, and the tropical forests are being felled at an alarming rate.

When these areas are cleared by heavy machinery, or if the ground is constantly used for piece-meal agriculture, the forest is never able to return to its original state, for the trees take many years to grow – even if they are

A victim of oil pollution.

allowed to – and their seeds may no longer be in the soil.

Then there is the pollution caused by chemicals. This too is having a bad effect on wild life. All over the world farmers are using sprays and chemical fertilizers. These drain through the soil into the streams and rivers, polluting them. Unfortunately fish and other water creatures are easily killed by these chemicals.

Industrial cities still use rivers as rubbish tips, and even the sea is being affected by the chemicals and sewage brought down by the rivers. We used to think that the life of the oceans would never be changed, but nowadays we find that dramatic changes are taking place. Over-intensive fishing means that the numbers of fish are being reduced, though the various nations are now trying to make sure that the nets the fishermen use allow the young fish to go free.

In the cold waters of the polar seas those large sea mammals, the whales, are hunted by man for their oily blubber and meat, and it is only by recent international agreement that there is at last a possibility of saving them from extinction.

The final responsibility

Unfortunately many creatures are in danger of

We have a beautiful and diverse world to live in. It is well worth looking after it with all the care we can. This is the task God himself has given us to do.

extinction, especially on islands where crowds of people live. Information about the rare and vanishing plants and animals is being collected and published by the International Union for the Conservation of Nature, so that we shall be able to know how best to look after them and save them from extinction.

Man has upset the balance of nature, and we must try to do something about this.

The opening chapter of this book reminded us that God gave man dominion over the created world, setting him here as his manager. We are in charge – with all the resources of the natural world at our disposal to develop and use.

But we must not forget the other side of the coin – that we are responsible and accountable to God for what we do. Surely this means – at the very lowest – that we have no right to allow or encourage the extermination of the different kinds of plants and animals with which we share this world. On the contrary, we should do all we can to conserve and care for every part of nature. We must ensure that these creatures and their essential environment not only survive but flourish in the way God intended. The greatest of the many wonders of creation – that we are the product of a loving God puts us under a natural obligation to be like him, loving and caring for the world – his world – that surrounds us.

Acknowledgements

Text
Articles on pages 21, 37, 55, 67, 77, 90, and 108 are based on scripts originally produced for broadcasting by Radio Worldwide and are used by kind permission.

Photographs
Cover: Butterfly feeding, Oxford Scientific Films Ltd; Hermit crab, Heather Angel; Satellite picture, Camera Press Ltd; Eclipse of the sun, Barnaby's Picture Library; Parakeet, Jean-Luc Ray; Mountain lion, Tony Stone Associates Ltd.

Camera Press Ltd: 9, 10, 11, 21, 24 (top L and R), 25, 44 (2, 3, 4), 45 (6, 7, 8), 62 (bottom), 84 (5, 6), 90 (bottom), 108 (top L), 110, 112, 118, 119, 121 (bottom R), end papers.

Heather Angel: 18 (bottom), 39 (L), 43, 45 (5), 57, 60, 74 (3, 4), 75 (5), 80 (top L), 82, 83, 85 (7), 87, 91 (R), 105 (4), 116–7, 122 (bottom R).

Barnaby's Picture Library: 7, 8, 14 (bottom), 32, 35, 44 (1), 48, 49, 62 (top), 70, 74 (1), 86, 90 (top), 114, 117 (R).

Oxford Scientific Films Ltd: 12, 14 (middle), 18 (top), 20, 31, 46, 59 (bottom R), 67, 88, 89, 91, 102, 105 (6), 106, 107 (R), 111 (L).

Tony Stone Associates Ltd: 14 (top), 26–7, 28, 29 (top), 59 (top), 64–5, 68, 78 (top), 78–9, 95, 97 (top), 108 (bottom L), 109, 123 (top R).

Natural History Photographic Agency: 59 (bottom L), 64 (bottom L), 65 (bottom L), 69, 84 (1, 2), 85 (3, 4), 104 (1), 105 (3, 5), 107 (L), 117 (bottom L).

Phil Manning/Richard Atwill: 19, 38, 39 (R), 47, 75 (6, 7, 8), 80 (bottom L), 97, 99 (bottom L), 108 (R), 115, 122 (bottom L).

A. J. Deane: 29 (bottom), 64 (R), 65 (R), 73, 74 (2), 75 (10), 80 (top R), 94 (R), 104 (2), 120 (bottom), 122 (top), 123 (top L).

David Alexander: 37, 54, 55 (top), 71, 111 (R).

F. N. Hepper: 58, 75 (9), 120–1, 121.

Institute of Geological Sciences: 24 (bottom), 50 (top L and R). NERC copyright. Reproduced by permission of the Director.

Jean-Luc Ray: 80 (bottom R), 123 (bottom R).

M. B. Waldron: 52, 53.

British Museum: 30 (bottom).

British Museum (Natural History): 55 (bottom).

Colorific: 116 (L). Bob Gomel © Time Inc. 1974.

De Beers Consolidated Mines Ltd: 50 (bottom).

Mary Evans Picture Library: 21 (bottom).

J. M. Flegg: 94 (L).

Meteorological Office/NCAR, Colorado: 66.

Arthur Oglesby: 93.

T. J. Stevenson: 99 (top).

James Webb: 36.

David and Jill Wright: 78 (middle).

Graphics
Tony Cantale: 9, 13, 17, 22, 32, 34, 36, 40, 41, 52, 61, 63, 69, 70, 77, 79, 81, 92–3, 98, 99, 115, 119.

Nicholas Rous: 29, 33, 35, 42, 46, 51, 56, 57, 62, 68, 76, 78, 86, 88, 91, 92 (top), 93, 95, 100, 102, 109, 110.